A STUDY OF ECONOMIC IMPACT

THE UNIVERSITY OF STIRLING

To my Father, and the memory of my Mother

A STUDY OF ECONOMIC IMPACT

THE UNIVERSITY OF STIRLING

MARK BROWNRIGG
Department of Economics
The University, Stirling

A HALSTED PRESS BOOK

JOHN WILEY & SONS
NEW YORK

Published by
Scottish Academic Press Ltd
25 Perth Street, Edinburgh 3
and distributed by
Chatto & Windus Ltd
40 William IV Street
London W.C.2

First published 1974

Published in the U.S.A. by Halsted Press,
a Division of John Wiley & Sons, Inb. New York

Library of Congress Cataloging in Publication Data

Brownrigg, Mark.
A study of economic impact: the University of Stirling.

"A Halsted Press book."
A revision of the author's thesis, University of Stirling.
Bibliography: p.
1. Community and college—Economic aspects—Stirling, Scotland. 2. Stirling, Scotland. University.
I. Title.
LC238.4.G73S742 1974 330.9 413′6081 73–224O3
ISBN–470–11365–0.

Printed in Great Britain by R. & R. Clark Ltd, Edinburgh

PREFACE

When it was first suggested to me that I should rework my doctorate thesis into a more generalised version for publication in book form, my reaction was considerably less than enthusiastic. To some extent, this was due to the prospect of returning to a completed piece of research. However, it was also based on a feeling that the material of the Stirling study might be too specialised to interest more than a few local planners and other economists working in the regional field.

However, when the University of Stirling released the results of my work to the press, I was taken aback completely by the sheer volume of correspondence which followed. I found myself facing many requests for further information on both my results and the methodology I had used, from a wide range of persons and bodies. The effect of this correspondence and the interest expressed during subsequent discussions with local planning officers and others concerned with regional planning and policy matters, was to tip the balance in favour of reworking the material of the thesis.

It must be made clear, however, that at no stage has this book ever been intended or designed to be a definitive survey of the various methods available in Regional Science by which economic impact can be studied. This is not a textbook of economic impact analysis. Rather, its purpose is to generalise some of the models used in my study of the University of Stirling, and to illustrate how this basic approach can be carried out in similar studies elsewhere. If the methodology used in the Stirling case study proves to be useful to others, then this book has achieved its end.

I should like to thank Professor C. V. Brown for the help he has given me while completing the book; not only did he provide much of the initial impetus towards publication which was, sadly, lacking in the author, but he has taken time to read and comment on an earlier draft of the work. I am also indebted greatly to my colleague Dr. M. A. Greig who, in addition to his assistance during the original thesis, has taken further time to read and criticise much of the present text of the book. Since the book is based on my thesis, I should like to acknowledge again the assistance of colleagues and others who helped me in the original work – in particular the valuable guidance of both Professor A. D. Bain and Dr. D. R. F. Simpson. I acknowledge, gratefully, the financial assistance offered in connection with the publication of the book by both the Carnegie Trust for the Universities of Scotland and the University of Stirling itself. I am also grateful for the permission of the Editors of the *Scottish Journal of Political Economy* to use some of the material of my articles in this work.

Last, and possibly most of all, I should like to thank my wife, who accepted (fairly) philosophically the prospect of her husband taking up yet more time from his family to convert a thesis into book form. Without her support, I doubt whether I could have weathered the various crises which have afflicted both pieces of work.

CONTENTS

1

Introduction

Any major new project which is introduced to a local economy will create a number of planning and other problems for the receiving region. The extent of these problems will depend upon the nature of the new project and the nature of the local economy in question.

The influence of a large new firm or institution is likely to extend considerably further than the mere direct employment offered by it to the local labour market. In purely employment terms, the expenditure pressure of these direct employees is likely to generate further indirect employment in the Services sector of the local economy. A further source of possible employment, normally more short term in nature, may be found in the increase in construction activity, both in constructing the premises of the original firm and in expanding capacity in both private and public sectors, if the existing level of capacity in the region is inadequate to cope with demand pressures arising from the project. Depending on the nature of the project, its development may build up local inter-industry trade flows, where it uses or provides inputs associated with local industries; if the new firm stimulates a significant increase in these trade flows, further employment could well be generated in other industries.

Apart from its impact on employment, the increase in economic activity associated with the new project could result in a considerable increase in local income levels, raising the prosperity of the area and possibly changing the nature of its infrastructure, especially if it stimulates considerable construction work. Rising local prosperity levels and an improved infrastructure could well attract further new entrants, with further interaction between employment and income.

Depending on the extent to which the local labour market can meet the demands for the various types of employment, another effect of growth resulting from the introduction of a large new project could be to create a fair sized inflow of immigrants to the region. This new source of population growth could have considerable effects on the spatial demands within the region. In the short term, spatial demands will reflect the immediate pressures of coping with an inflow of population and meeting its demands for both capital and consumer goods. In the longer term, the age structure of the immigrants might diverge sufficiently from the established pattern to influence local birth and death rates, so changing any forecasts made of long run population growth.

A second main influence on the economic impact of any new project will be the characteristics of the receiving region. If the local economy's industrial structure has suffered a long term decline, the introduction of even a major new source of employment may do little more than merely prop up current low levels of income, employment and population. If, on the other hand, the receiving region has a viable economy, with a well diversified industrial structure and reasonably high levels of income and employment, the effects of the new project can be considerable. It may even act as a catalyst in securing further rapid growth in the economy.

In most cases, the degree of economic impact will lie between these two extremes. However, without knowledge of the local economy, it is difficult to predict the extent of the impact. Indeed, without knowledge of the local economy, it becomes difficult to assess whether internal forces and the new project are complementary, or competing sources of growth, when each will impose constraints on the other.

Any study of economic impact must therefore have two lines of examination. The first must analyse the receiving region to determine whether this will support or hinder the growth from the new project. The second must, in turn, analyse the nature of the new project and provide estimates of the likely demands for employment stemming from this, so that any implications for prosperity and population can be studied.

This book has two main related objectives. The first objective is to analyse the economic impact of a new University on its local economy. While the University of Stirling is different in nature from the more normal type of new firm, it employs considerable numbers of academic and other staff. The expenditure of these and the student body attending the University places considerable pressure on the local economy. Looked at in this way, the establishment of a new University is the equivalent of introducing a major new industry to the local economy. It is at least possible that the economic consequences of this siting decision will be considerable. If this is shown to be the case then, with the current wave of expansion in University and other educational institutions, these economic consequences should be considered as a further factor in any policy decisions.

The second main objective of the book is to develop a basic model from which estimates can be made of impact on income, employment and population. In its initial stages, this involved the construction of a modified regional income multiplier model, with a series of minor techniques by which the resultant income estimates could be translated into employment and population terms. While this evolved in terms of the University of Stirling, it became apparent that the information inputs could be based on many other types of new project, and the basic University models used to provide similar estimates for these. Therefore the second objective developed into providing an operational model based on the regional income multiplier approach, which could be used elsewhere to provide guidance to physical planners and others concerned.

Throughout the book, then, the analysis of the economic impact of the University of Stirling is presented as a case study which illustrates the various techniques of analysis. It is hoped that this approach will simultaneously indicate the extent of economic impact which might be expected from a major new project, and the various methods by which any such project can be analysed.

The outline of the book is as follows. In Chapter 2, the population characteristics of the Stirling Study Area are analysed and the various pre-University trends identified for later use. Chapter 3 examines the local industrial structure and the employment characteristics of the local labour market. The information gathered on population trends is used, in Chapter 4, to provide projections of the internal growth of population for the region, i.e. the growth which is likely to take place irrespective of the effects of the University. Chapter 5 performs a similar exercise, using the earlier information on local industrial structure in conjunction with national forecasts to project the internal changes in employment which are likely to occur.

The next series of Chapters illustrate how the growth forces of the new project can be analysed. In Chapter 6, the current literature on the regional multiplier is examined and, from this, is developed a basic model suitable for operational use in a regional situation. The various terms in the model are quantified for the University case study in Chapter 7 and the model used to provide estimates of the impact of the project on local incomes. Using this data and a modified employment multiplier, further estimates are then made of the indirect employment generated in the local service industries by the growth of the project. In Chapter 8, the overall employment figures from the growth of the project are analysed, to provide a basis from which estimates can be made of the impact of the new project and its secondary growth on local population levels.

Throughout, the conclusions are summarised at the end of each Chapter with, in Chapter 9, the estimates for both internal and University growth gathered together, so that their implications for planning in the Stirling Study Area can be considered. Finally, in Chapter 10, the various main conclusions are drawn together, both with respect to the economic impact of the new University on its local economy and, equally, the viability of this type of approach for similar studies of economic impact elsewhere.

2

Population

The purpose of studying this aspect of the region's economy is to gain some understanding of the present and possible future characteristics of the indigenous population. This implies that the purpose of the exercise is not merely to provide a present description of the area. Where it is intended to make a series of projections of the area's population, then the detail of the model which will be designed for this will also depend upon the information gathered. It is necessary therefore not only to analyse the present characteristics of the population but also to attempt to explain why these characteristics have developed.

A simple analysis of population characteristics is possible based on the various Census of Population returns and the Annual Reports of the Registrar General.[1] Both of these sources provide population statistics in sufficient geographical detail to allow the computation of overall totals for any reasonable size of Study Area, even where this does not coincide with county, or larger area boundaries. Analysis of this data for a period of 10 to 15 years prior to the commencement of work on the project should provide sufficient information on the internal characteristics of the region. For example, the period chosen for the analysis of the Stirling Study Area was 1951–66. This latter year represented not only a convenient Census date, but was also the year in which the opening of the University of Stirling in 1967 was announced; effectively it was the last year in which no influence could be attributed to the University.

Having determined the period of the analysis, the next step is to select the type of information required. While information needs will obviously vary, data can be usefully gathered and analysed on aspects such as the total population size of the region, its geographical dispersion within the region, its age and sex structure, and its past trends of growth and decline. For the purpose of making population projections at a later stage, some attempt must be made at providing further information on why the observed changes have taken place, so that some judgement can be made of whether the

[1] Full Census reports are available for the postwar years 1951, 1961 and are in the process of being published for 1971; the 1966 Census was based on a 10% sample of population. The County Tables of the Census in question will provide the population data for the various Local Authority areas, as will the population estimates, births and deaths figures in the Annual Reports of the Registrar-General.

observed trends will continue, be modified, or alter completely in the future. In particular, some analysis must be made of the size and nature of the migration flows experienced by the region. Not only will these augment or deplete directly the present population base of the region, but their impact on the age structure and sex balance will also influence the rate of growth of population in the future.[2]

This chapter illustrates the use of these simple techniques in relation to the analysis of the population base of the Stirling Study Area, and comments on how the results can be gathered to provide the necessary knowledge of this aspect of the region. In Chapter 4, it is shown how much of this same information can be used in making population projections for the future internal growth of the area.

The Population of the Study Area

In terms of total population, the Stirling Study Area increased in size from 88,267 persons in 1951, to 92,800 persons in 1961 and 95,577 persons in June 1966. To obtain some relative standard for this 8·2% increase over the period, it can be contrasted to the 1·9% increase in total population over the same period for Scotland. Breaking down these figures into intercensal changes, the Study Area population increased by 5·1% as against the Scottish increase of 1·6% between 1951–61, and by 3·0% against the Scottish increase of 0·2% for the period 1961–66. This seems to indicate that the Study Area's population has risen consistently at a much higher rate than the Scotland figures, a trend which can be confirmed by an examination of earlier Census returns. Secondly, the figures suggest that the rate of population growth in the Study Area accelerated slightly over the first six years of the 1960's, in comparison with Scotland, where it slowed down markedly.

The geographical distribution of the population within the boundaries of the Study Area is shown in Table 2.1. The two main urban centres of Stirling and Alloa accounted for 40,672, or 46·1% of the total population at the beginning of the period and 42,061 persons, or 44·0% of the total population at the end of the period. The next two largest concentrations of population were the rural Districts of County of Alloa D.C. and Central No. 1 D.C., which between them accounted for a further 27,937 persons, or 31·7% of the total population in 1951 and 32,000 persons, or 33·9% of the total population in 1966. The remaining 20% of the population of the Study Area was distributed over the small burghs of Alva, Dollar, Tillicoultry, Doune, Dunblane and Bridge of Allan, and the small rural Hillfoots D.C.[3]

[2] See the effect of varying the migration net flow assumptions in the population projections of Chapter 4.

[3] The populations for Dollar and Bridge of Allan have been stated throughout as net of the resident students of Dollar Academy and the Beacon School for girls. From Census

This distribution indicates a fairly rural type of area, which is confirmed if the various Census returns are used to calculate population density per acre. The figures of about 12 persons per acre for Alloa and about 10 persons per acre for Stirling are completely offset by the large rural Districts of County, where the most heavily populated, Alloa D.C., has only 1·1 persons per acre, Central No. 1, 0·4 per acre and the Hillfoots 0·2 per acre. Overall, the population density for the Study Area over the period has been steady at 1·1 persons per acre.

Over the period almost all parts of the Study Area have increased in terms of population. The largest single increase was of 3,823 persons for Alloa D.C. This was almost entirely caused over the early 1950's by the influx of miners from the North Lanarkshire coal fields to the mines of the new Alloa area.[4] This same influx can be traced in the population increases for Stirling, Alloa and Tillicoultry. While the main population increases over the period 1951–61 can be explained in terms of this single immigration source, the population increases over the period 1961–66 were of a rather different nature. During this later period, immigration appears to have been associated with a wave of housing development, mainly for owner-occupiers, this being concentrated around Stirling, Alloa, Dollar, Tillicoultry, Bridge of Allan and Dunblane. This particular phase of development of the area appears to have taken the nature of a commuter belt residential zone for Glasgow, Edinburgh, Falkirk and Grangemouth.[5] However, taking the period as a whole, the various changes in population over the period have had little more than a marginal effect on its geographical distribution within the boundaries of the Study Area.

In dealing with age structure, if comparison is again desired with some national standard, Census data will normally allow the necessary tables to be constructed, either in terms of 5-year age groups, or the broader 0–14, 15–64, '65 and over' groups, for males and females. If all that is needed, however, is broad guidance on whether the Study Area is relatively older or younger than some average figure, then this can be measured quite simply and clearly by using the 'age index'[6] approach. This device has the virtue of allowing simple comparison both of one area over time and between areas. For example, the age index of the Stirling Study Area rose from 31·3 to 33·1 between 1951 and

---

figures there were 226 of these at Dollar and 31 at Bridge of Allan in 1966; the 1951 Census was during vacation when there were no students.

[4] 9 new mines were opened here from 1951 to 1956; however, 4 old mines closed over the same period, followed by 6 more in the early 1960's. By 1963, not a single pit in Clackmannan County was producing coal; even Glenochil, the major new colliery, had been closed – *Third Statistical Account of Scotland, Stirling and Clackmannan*, pp. 433–50.

[5] Based on information given by builders to the planning officers of the various burghs in the area.

[6] The age index is the percentage of persons in the population aged 45 and over.

[7] The full Census years of 1951 and 1961 have been used, since the 1966 Sample Census does not provide sufficient detail, even in unpublished form, to permit this analysis.

1966; this indicates that the area's age structure had become marginally older. The Scottish age index rose from 32·4 to 35·2 over the same period; the Stirling Study Area was both relatively younger and ageing less rapidly than Scotland as a whole. Equally, the age index can be applied to component parts of the Study Area. For the Stirling Study Area, the index varies from declining areas such as Doune (47·6), or retirement catchment areas such as Bridge of Allan (43·4) to, at the other extreme, rural areas such as Central No. 1 D.C. (28·3). Again, the index can be used to illustrate clearly the effects of commuter immigration over the period on Dunblane (47·4 to 34·6) and Tillicoultry (33·7 to 27·4).

However, in many cases, such comparisons may be of little more than academic interest. Here, the really necessary data on age structure and sex can be gathered and observed in the form of intercensal tables such as Table 2.2. This shows that between 1951 and 1961 there was an increase of 2,512 males overall, due mainly to increases in the age ranges 5–19 and 45–64, with increases of 1,770 and 1,584 respectively. Again, there was an overall increase of 2,053 females over the period, concentrated mainly in the same age ranges, with 1,245 for the 5–19 and 1,354 for the 45–64-year-old age range. The figures show that this was offset by a significant net loss of population in the age range 20–44 of 830 males and 1,152 females; this would appear to indicate an outward migration flow over these age groups, which is typical of the Scottish pattern.

In both Census years, for all 5-year age groups from 20 years of age onwards, there were more females than males. For the age range above 60 years of age, this is consistent with the effect of heavier male mortality rates over this range, particularly in an area where there appeared to be a steady stream of immigrants for retiral to the area. Over the 20–59 age range, this was probably due not so much to differing mortality rates as the wide nature of female employment in the Study Area[8] in both manufacturing and service industries.

Migration Patterns in the Study Area

The earlier section of the chapter showed that the population of the Study Area increased steadily over both intercensal periods at a rate significantly greater than for Scotland as a whole and that, indeed, there was some evidence that the rate of population increase had risen over the 1961–66 period. This difference in the behaviour of population growth between the Study Area and Scotland could have been caused by differences in birth and death rates or by differences in migration patterns. This section of the chapter examines natural increase and migration behaviour in more detail.

[8] See the analysis of employment in Chapter 3.

Comparison of birth and death rates[9] for any given year is not satisfactory, particularly where one of the areas is relatively small, like the Study Area. The approach taken here has been to average the rates over the two intercensal periods. The average birth rate for the Study Area over 1951–61 was 18·8 as against the Scottish average rate of 18·4, but, for 1961–66, the Scottish rate of 19·7 was higher than the Study Area rate of 19·3. On the other hand, the average death rate for both periods was lower in the Study Area, 11·3 as against the Scottish rate of 11·9 for 1951–61 and 11·4 as against 12·2 for 1961–66. Given that there was no significant difference in birth rates and only a slightly lower death rate in the Study Area, there has been nothing in the rate of natural increase to provide an explanation for the differences in the rate of population growth.

While there was little difference between the rates of the Study Area as a whole and Scotland, there were considerable, if predictable, differences between sections of the Study Area and also between the two time periods in some sections. The older, declining or retiral type of burgh, such as Doune, Dunblane, Dollar and Bridge of Allan, all showed much lower birth rates than the Study Area average, being in the 13·0 to 17·0 range. However, the effects of the population influx of 1961–66 showed up clearly with, in particular, the intercensal average birth rate rising from 13·1 to 25·0 in Dunblane and 15·4 to 20·4 in Bridge of Allan. Death rates, on the other hand, varied rather less both between sections and over time.

With no significant differences in the patterns of natural increase, the differing rates of population growth are therefore likely to have been caused by differing patterns of migration. Migration flows can be analysed in two stages. Firstly, it is a fairly simple matter to estimate the direction of the net migration flow and the volume of this. Secondly, if it is desired, further estimates can be made of the impact of the migration flows on the age structure of the population.

There is no readily available data which will allow estimates to be made of the gross migration flows into and out of a region. Analysis can therefore only show the net balance, i.e. the net gain or net loss, of the gross flows. A simple method of estimating the net migration flow for a region is to take its statistics for births and deaths, as published by the Registrar-General, adjust these for normal residence, compute the natural increase over the period, and compare this to the actual increase, as calculated from the Census returns at the beginning and the end of the period.[10] Where the natural increase exceeds the actual increase, there has been net migration outwards; where the actual increase exceeds the natural increase, there has been net migration inwards.

[9] These rates are per 1,000 of population, corrected for usual residence – Annual Reports of the Registrar-General for Scotland, years 1951–57, tables 5 and 6; 1958 onwards, table 7.

[10] The Census reports are taken in April, with births and deaths given for the full year; the first and last years must be adjusted for this.

Using this approach for the Stirling Study Area, it was estimated[11] that there had been a net migration loss of about 2,700 persons, or 3·0% of its 1951 population over 1951–61, and about 900 persons, or 1·0% of its 1961 population over 1961–66. In comparison, Scotland had a net migration loss of 5·0% of its population for 1951–61 and 3·6% for 1961–66. These figures confirm that the different rates of population growth were attributable to the patterns of emigration. Not only did the Stirling Study Area have a lower rate of net migration loss over the period, but there is also evidence that for 1961–66, the rate of loss declined for the Study Area, whereas it increased for Scotland as a whole.

Finally, it may be felt necessary to make some estimates of the effects of the migration patterns on the age structure of the population of the Study Area. The simple approach used above can be extended to estimate the net flows by age group for the area.[12] This time, the full age structure of the population for the base year is taken from the Census report. Then, for each year, from the Annual Report of the Registrar-General, births are added to and deaths deducted from the various age groups in the population; the survivors are then 'aged' by one year and the process repeated till the end of the period. The resultant figures for the end of the period show, from the natural increase figures, what the population's age structure would have been in the absence of any migration flows. This estimated population is then compared with the actual population given by the Census report for the end of the period, and the net migration loss or gain calculated for each age group.[13]

This approach, applied to the Study Area, indicates that,[14] over the period 1951–61, there was a heavy net loss of population over the age range 15–44 of about 3,000 persons, mainly concentrated on the 15–34 section of the range. This would be a fairly typical age pattern for migrants and the loss of their child dependants would provide some explanation for the net loss of about 700 in the 5–9 age group. Heavy losses in these age groups were experienced by all parts of the Study Area. To offset the losses, there was a smaller net gain of about 350[15] persons in the age range 45–64: geographically, this inflow was concentrated on the areas receiving the inflow of miners, who

[11] See Table 2.3, page 12.

[12] This type of model is discussed fully and used in *The Lothians Regional Survey and Plan*, chapter 3, B. M. Swift.

[13] While this approach is very simple in essence, it can involve a fair amount of repetitive calculation, working as it does on an annual adjustment basis. The same results can be estimated more quickly by the zero migration type of population projection model discussed in Chapter 4. The Census data of 1951 can be taken as the base population, the fertility and mortality rates based on births and deaths data for the period, with the projected population compared with the actual Census population for 1961, or 1966.

[14] See Table 2.4, page 13.

[15] In fact, the net gain was rather greater than this, if computed from the smaller burghs and Alloa D.C.; it was reduced by very heavy outflows from the rural D.C.'s, particularly Central No. 1, which might reflect the pattern of redundancies in the agricultural rundown over this period (based on conversation with D.E.P. officials).

seem to have been spread over the range 35–54; the rest of the net inflow was spread over the 'retirement' areas. The main compensating net inflow for the period was in the 0–14 age range, the largest part of which was probably the child dependants brought into the area by the older immigration inflow. The estimated net loss of population for the '65 and over' group was probably due in part to the assumptions made about the age distribution of mortality rates, as well as the continuation of the net loss trend observed in rural districts for the 45–64 group.

The estimates of the effect of migration for the 1961–66 period are further complicated by the fact that the 1966 Census was based on a 10% sample, which created difficulties in estimating the appropriate population parameters from which the migration flows could be deduced.[16] However, it would seem that, over the period, there was a net loss through emigration of over 1,000 persons in the age range 15–44, this loss being concentrated on Alloa D.C., Stirling, and Central No. 1 D.C. There is some evidence that the loss which would normally be expected in this age range was augmented by the series of mining closures in the area. There was also a loss of about 400 persons in the '45 and over' age range, but this is not significant statistically. There was no real gain or loss in the 0–14 age group. Again the more detailed analysis supports earlier discussion by showing that the gains over the period were in Dollar, Dunblane and Bridge of Allan mainly; this time, however, they were clearly in the 'under 45' groups, indicating a commuter type of residential development rather than immigration to retirement, although this latter source of inflow was still in evidence.[17]

Overall, the estimates of the effect of migration on the age structure of the Study Area provide some evidence that the migration pattern in both periods has been one of a two way flow. To offset the normal Scottish pattern of loss in the 'under 40' range, there has been an immigration inflow over the period. While there is no clear-cut method of estimating the gross flows which have occurred, it would seem that the inflow experienced in the Study Area was of persons in relatively older age groups than those hit by emigration, and their child dependants. This was particularly true of the 1951–61 period. Secondly, the falling rate of net loss of population for 1961–66 would seem to have been caused by an increased inflow to the smaller residential burghs; the model's estimates indicate that this inflow was, on average, 10–15 years younger than the inflow recorded for the previous period.

In conclusion, the population characteristics of the Study Area which have been analysed in this chapter have shown that the rate of population increase in the Study Area has consistently exceeded the rate for Scotland as a whole. Overall, the population of the Study Area was marginally younger than the

[16] The net outflows for these districts all lie outside the range of standard error at a 95% level of confidence.

[17] The results are summarised in Table 2.5, page 13.

Scottish pattern, although this appears to have had little effect on relative birth rates; while the death rate in the Study Area was slightly lower, this could reflect, in addition to the younger nature of the population, the predominantly rural nature of the area. Despite the higher rate of population increase, there was a heavy loss over the period of younger persons from the Study Area. Finally, to offset emigration losses from the Study Area, there has been, over the period, a significant inflow of older persons, recently augmented by the considerable house construction development in the area.

Table 2.1

Distribution of Population within the Stirling Study Area, 1951 and 1966

	1951		*1966*		*Change 1951–66*
	Persons	%	*Persons*	%	*Persons*
Clackmannan					
Alloa	13,521	15·3	14,046	14·7	+525
Alva	4,106	4·6	3,996	4·2	−110
Dollar	1,389	1·6	1,943	2·0	+554
Tillicoultry	3,876	4·4	4,082	4·3	+206
Alloa D.C.	11,377	12·9	15,200	15·9	+3,823
Hillfoots D.C.	3,263	3·7	3,050	3·2	−213
Perth					
Doune	834	0·9	776	0·8	−58
Dunblane	3,017	3·4	3,500	3·7	+483
Stirling					
Stirling	27,151	30·8	28,015	29·3	+864
Bridge of Allan	3,173	3·6	3,769	3·9	+596
Central No. 1 D.C.	16,560	18·8	17,200	18·0	+640
Study Area	88,267	100·0	95,577	100·0	+7,310

Source: Census, Scotland 1951 and Annual Report of the Registrar-General for Scotland, 1966.

Table 2.2

Population by Age Groups, 1951 and 1961

Age Groups	*Males* 1951	*Males* 1961	*Inter-censal change*	*Females* 1951	*Females* 1961	*Inter-censal change*
0–4	4,536	4,491	−45	4,273	4,311	+38
5–9	3,629	3,958	+329	3,532	3,757	+225
10–14	3,406	4,418	+1,012	3,357	4,218	+861
15–19	2,949	3,378	+429	3,196	3,355	+159
20–4	2,903	2,692	−211	3,422	3,062	−360
25–9	3,226	2,872	−354	3,486	2,903	−583
30–4	2,968	2,886	−82	3,099	3,146	+47
35–9	3,033	3,102	+69	3,295	3,241	−54
40–4	3,091	2,839	−252	3,255	3,053	−202
45–9	2,874	2,905	+31	3,075	3,149	+74
50–4	2,377	2,881	+504	2,760	3,098	+338
55–9	1,885	2,609	+724	2,400	2,795	+395
60–4	1,616	1,924	+308	2,104	2,402	+298
65–9	1,425	1,378	−47	1,772	2,005	+233
70–4	1,058	1,036	−22	1,487	1,565	+78
75 and over	1,157	1,260	+103	1,621	2,111	+490
Total	42,133	44,629	+2,496	46,134	48,171	+2,037

Source: Census 1951, Vol. 1, parts 13, 26, 31, table 15.
Census 1961, Vol. 1, parts 13, 26, 31, table 6.

Table 2.3

Estimates of Migration, 1951–66

	Study Area 1951–61	*Study Area* 1961–66	*Scotland* 1951–61	*Scotland* 1961–66
Census population	88,267	92,830	5,096,415	5,178,490
Births over period	17,405	9,462	953,652	513,209
Deaths ,,	10,192	5,396	618,399	316,545
Natural increase over period	7,213	4,066	335,253	196,664
Actual ,,	4,533	3,180	82,075	12,310
Migration ,,	−2,680	−890	−253,178	−184,354
as % base population	−3·0%	−1·0%	−5·0%	−3·6%

Table 2.4

Estimates of Effect of Migration on Study Area Age Structure 1951–61

	Population 1961	*Gain/Loss*	*As % of Population*
0–4	8,802	+1,169	+13%
5–9	7,797	−687	−9%
10–14	8,554	+263	+3%
15–24	12,487	−1,483	−12%
25–34	11,807	−1,049	−9%
35–44	12,235	−401	−3%
45–54	12,033	+339	+3%
55–64	9,730	+17	0
65–74	5,984	−530	−9%
75 and over	3,371	−148	−4%
Total	92,800	−2,510	−3%

Table 2.5

Estimates of Effect of Migration on Study Area Age Structure 1961–66

	Population 1966	*Gain/Loss*	*As % of Population*
0–14	26,250	−40	0%
15–44	37,980	−1,210	−3%
45 and over	31,780	−380	−1%
Total	96,010	−1,630	−2%

3

Industrial Structure and Employment

It is necessary to analyse the industrial structure of the region not merely to provide some descriptive information about the pattern of employment and output, but also to allow an assessment to be made of how the region will absorb the new project. How well diversified is the region's industrial structure and to what extent, if at all, will the new industry's labour and other needs differ from those of established local industries? To what extent can local industries expect to be involved in and benefit from the trade flows generated by the new industry? Will the local services base be adequate to support a major new development? Do sufficient supplies of either skilled or trainable labour reserves exist to permit both indigenous growth and the growth of the new industry? Answers to all of these questions must be based on sound knowledge of the local industrial structure.

If it is intended to make any projections of the local pattern of employment, it is essential that the past trends of growth and decline in the various local industries must be identified and analysed. As with population, the analysis must not merely show what has happened but, for the purposes of the projections, also explain why the observed changes have taken place. In the context of changes in local industrial structure, the analysis must attempt to show the extent to which these were influenced by national experience on the one hand and purely local characteristics on the other. Finally, the information provided must be such that some judgement can be formed as to whether the trends observed for the past will apply unchanged to, or must be modified for, the future.

The gathering of statistics for the local industrial structure is rather more difficult than was the case for population. While some Census publications do contain employment data on a local authority basis[1] this is not generally adequate, being too irregular a series and, in most cases, being based on a small percentage sample of households. By far the best series available is the employment returns of the Department of Employment, but it is unlikely that the published data from this source will relate to the Study Area, unless this has been defined to coincide with planning region boundaries. In most

[1] This data can be found in the special Economic Activity, Occupation and Workplace tables for the Census. For the 1971 Census, some of these tables may, ultimately, be provided on the basis of a 100% sample, for an extra charge.

cases, application will have to be made to the Department of Employment for access to the unpublished returns of the local Employment Exchange offices. When this permission is given, some adjustments might have to be made to the statistics to bring the Employment Exchange area(s) into conformity with the local authority boundaries of the Study Area, since the geographical bases for Department of Employment and Census returns do not necessarily coincide.[2] A final problem is that, while the period chosen for analysis must be of sufficient duration to allow observation of trends, it is likely to be constrained by the periodic redefinition of S.I.C. Orders by the Department of Employment.[3]

The chapter analyses, firstly, the pattern of industrial structure in the Study Area at 1966. Secondly, it examines the trends of growth and decline which were experienced over the period, comparing local to national experience here and assessing the effect of these changes on male and female employment. Finally, an analysis is made of the state of the local labour market as measured through unemployment patterns and activity rates. The construction of employment projections is discussed in Chapter 5.

The Pattern of Industry

The industrial structure of the Study Area as at 1961 and 1966 is shown in Table 3.1. In general terms, it can be seen that the local area was rather more dependent on its Primary industries (S.I.C. Orders I and II) than the Scottish economy as a whole, with local employment in these amounting to 10·3% of the total labour force in comparison with the national figure of 6·2% for 1966. With a roughly similar dependence on the group of Manufacturing industries (S.I.C. Orders III to XVIII), the effect of this emphasis on Primary industries has been to leave the Services sector (Orders XIX to XXIV), despite its considerable growth over the period, significantly smaller than the national pattern, employing 42·4% against the national 48·6% of the total labour force.

In terms of the full list of S.I.C. Orders, a fair number of differences can be observed in the relative patterns of employment. This is inevitable. It is highly unlikely that a small sub-region will have all its industries developed to

[2] In the Stirling case study, the area covered by the joint returns of the two local employment offices overlapped the Census Local Authority areas in several places; the statistics had therefore to be reduced on the basis of employment data (unpublished) from the 1966 Census and discussions with the managers of the Employment offices of workplaces sited in the overlap areas.

[3] The period chosen for the Stirling Study Area was 1961 to 1966. If the period had been extended to 1951–66, serious comparison problems would have arisen from the 1958 redefinition of Orders. The employment figures throughout are given in terms of the 1958 S.I.C. classification. Finally, the use of Census years 1961 and 1966 permits some comparison with Census returns.

the same extent as the national pattern. Some industries such as, for the Stirling Study Area, Metal Manufacturing or Shipbuilding and Marine Engineering will be virtually missing, whereas others, e.g. Mining or Textiles, being regional specialisms, play a rather more important part in the pattern of employment.

The six largest industries in the Stirling local economy at June 1966 were Textiles, Professional and Scientific Services, Miscellaneous Services, Distributive Trades, Mining and Construction. While these were also the six largest in 1961, some changes took place in their ranking positions over the period. Mining declined from the largest single industry of 1961, when about 5,100 persons were employed, to the fifth largest, employing about 3,400 persons, by the end of the period. Professional Services, on the other hand, rose from 5th to 2nd largest, finally employing about 4,100 persons. There were no real changes in the ranking positions of the other main industries; Textiles, by virtue of the decline of Mining, became the largest industry with 4,200 persons employed, while the others remained as before, despite some increases in their labour forces.

In terms of location factors[4] in these major industries, Mining (3·30), Textiles (2·43) and Miscellaneous Services (1·15) were regional specialisms. While Construction (0·98) and Professional Services (0·91) were about the same relative size, Distributive Trades (0·73) was a rather less important source of employment in the Study Area than in the Scottish pattern.

Looking in more detail at these main industries in the Study Area, the largest, Textiles, was mainly concerned with the manufacture of woollens, worsteds, hosiery and knitted goods; given the nature of the industry, about 75% of the labour force were female. Employment in Professional Services was mainly in educational, medical and dental services, which again were female predominant (about 80% female). Miscellaneous Services consisted of employment in hotels and catering, car sales, garages and filling stations and private domestic service; overall, the female proportion was again predominant at about 60%. Distributive Trades, predictably, had about 90% of its labour force in retail distribution, with the remainder scattered over wholesale distribution, coal, builders' and agricultural merchants; again, under the influence of retail distribution, about 60% was female employment. Mining, on the other hand, was almost exclusively male employment and almost entirely (about 95%) concerned with coal mining. Finally, Construction was again almost exclusively male employment and was concerned

[4] Location factors are a more convenient method of comparing the relative importance of industries between areas; the L.F. for the Study Area in any industry is the percentage employed in that industry in the Study Area divided by the percentage employed in the same industry in Scotland. Where the L.F. value is greater than unity, it is a more important source of employment in the Study Area than in Scotland, i.e. it is a regional specialism, and conversely. Its main advantage is that it not only indicates specialisms, but gives a measure of the degree of specialism.

mainly with housebuilding; while civil engineering had provided several large labour intensive projects in the past, at that time there was a lull in this type of work.

Trends of Growth and Decline, 1961–66

This section analyses the changes which have taken place in the industrial structure of the Study Area over the period, with expansion and contraction measured in terms of numbers employed.[5] While, overall, there was only an increase of about 400 persons in the total labour force, individual industries experienced considerable changes over the period. The main employment increases were in Professional and Scientific Services (about 1,100), Miscellaneous Services (about 600), Construction (about 450), Gas, Electricity and Water (about 400), Bricks, Potteries and Glass (about 300) and Insurance, Banking and Finance (about 250). On the other hand, the industries suffering the main contraction in employment were Mining (about 1,750), Public Administration and Defence (about 550), Food, Drink and Tobacco (about 250), Agriculture (about 150) and Textiles (about 150).

Growth or decline in any industry will reflect the influence of both the national trend over the period and purely local experience. It is possible to make at least a rough estimate of the extent to which the changes recorded reflect these two components. To do so, the Scottish pattern of change over the period was applied to the industrial structure of the Study Area at the beginning of the period; this provided estimates of numbers employed by industry for the end of the period if the Study Area had conformed to the Scottish experience. When these estimates were compared with actual numbers employed at the end of the period, local residuals emerged, i.e. changes which could not be explained in terms of purely national experience.[6]

The estimates made show major local residuals of above national trend growth for the following industries.[7] Professional and Scientific Services had a residual of over 550 persons for the period, resulting from an increase of 38% in employment as against the Scottish figure of 19%. Growth in this industry was shared evenly between educational and medical services and was the result of substantial development of capacity in these parts of the public

[5] Description of industrial structure by employment figures is subject to two main weaknesses: firstly, at any moment of time it will understate the importance of capital intensive industries; secondly, in assessing changes in structure over time, technological changes obscure growth and decline estimates based on employment figures. However, to a small region, the important effects of changes in structure are their repercussions on local employment.

[6] The method also has two obvious weaknesses: firstly, it assumes that there is an identical pattern of employment between the Study Area and Scotland, i.e. L.F. = 1 in all industries and secondly it assumes an identical pattern of M.L.H. industry groups within each S.I.C. Order.

[7] See Table 3.2, page 25.

sector over the period, due in part to a coincidence in the timing of expenditure plans[8] as well as the growing needs of the area for these services over the 1960's. The second largest residual was recorded for Bricks, Potteries and Glass; while the main employment section here was concerned with the manufacture of glass containers for the Scottish market, the growth over the period was in the manufacture of abrasives and building materials to service local and Central belt construction work. The third main residual was of about 300 persons over the national trend in Gas, Electricity and Water; this reflected the expansion of electricity generation capacity at the Kincardine Power Station. The fourth largest residual was for Miscellaneous Services, which had a gain of about 250 persons over the trend; expansion here was almost entirely in the hotels and catering section, partly as a result of growth in the through tourist trade and partly as a result of the residential developments in the area. The final main residual was for Insurance, Banking and Finance, which increased employment by over 50% for the period; this was largely attributable to the siting of the headquarters of a large Scottish insurance concern at Stirling during the period. In all these cases, obviously, the location factor value for the industry increased over the period.

Almost all of the negative residuals, i.e. where growth was less than the national trend, were relatively insignificant. The largest residual here was for Public Administration and Defence, which had a short-fall of about 750 persons from the national trend. While to some extent this was caused by a reduction of manpower in local defence establishments, a part of the 'loss' was the result of local adjustments in industrial classification during the period, which transferred persons from this group to, mainly, Professional and Scientific Services.[9] To some extent, the same explanation applies to the only other main negative residual, for Food, Drink and Tobacco; part at least of the absolute decline in persons employed over the period was caused by another reclassification from this Order to Distributive Trades.[10]

However, this type of approach can tend to apply a national trend explanation to changes caused by local experiences in an industry. In mining there was a considerable run-down in manpower over the period of about 34%, which was reflected exactly in the Study Area, despite the fact that the latter had been designated as one of the few growth areas in Scotland for this industry. To some extent, the run-down in the Study Area was a true reflection of the national trend of closure of older, less efficient collieries. Despite these closures, in 1960 there were 13 active collieries in the Study Area, most of them recently opened, employing 4,800 men and producing between them 2 million tons per annum. Yet by 1963 only three of the smaller mines were

[8] Based on information given by the County planners. However, growth in this sector has been a little exaggerated by a local reclassification of industry – see later comments.

[9] It has been impossible to get further details on the numbers or type of labour involved.

[10] The transfer was from M.L.H. 231 to 810, mainly warehousing of malted whisky – again no details of numbers involved available.

producing coal[11] and employing only 1,500 men; since then, the balance of the labour force in the industry have been taken daily to coal fields outside the area, in Fife and West Lothian. This decline in employment was not so much a national trend effect as the result of an overoptimistic assessment of the quantity and quality of deposits, a series of mistakes which culminated in the closure of the new, large Glenochil Mine and the subsequent Public Inquiry.

A further analysis of industrial expansion over the period can be made by regrouping the various industries into two categories, one for regional specialisms, i.e. where location factors exceeded unity, and one for industries which were relatively less important to the Study Area, i.e. where the location factors were less than unity. This allows a grouping of the residuals to show that the section composed of regional specialisms expanded at slightly less than the national pattern had forecast, whereas the industries which were not important traditionally to the area had a significantly larger growth in employment than would have been expected from the national average.[12] The effects of the changes recorded for 1961–66 were to broaden the industrial base of the Study Area and, by doing so in the non-Manufacturing sector, bring the Services sector to nearer the Scottish pattern.

Finally, changes in industrial structure, particularly where they involved a marked growth in the Services sector relative to Manufacturing, were unlikely to affect male and female job opportunities equally. The 1·2% increase in total employment over the period was compounded of a 5% decline in males employed and a 12% increase in females employed. As a result of this, the proportion of males in the Study Area labour force fell from 63% in 1961 to 59% in 1966, with a corresponding rise in the female proportion from 37% to 41%. Growth of employment over the period was mainly in female employment, partly due to the heavy run-down in male predominant mining, but also partly due to the nature of the growth. S.I.C. Orders XX to XXIII offered new employment to 1,900 females; female employment in Distribution increased by about 300, in Insurance by about 200, in Professional and Scientific services by about 850 and in Miscellaneous services by about 550. Over the period, in no less than 14 Orders, the proportion of females employed relatively to males rose.

The State of the Labour Market

The previous section indicated that recent growth had tended to come from the less traditionally important local industries, thus broadening the industrial base of the Stirling Study Area. It also showed that these changes had affected the job opportunity pattern of male and female employment, tending

[11] Coal production was entirely for Kincardine Power Station in the surviving collieries All information here was given by N.C.B. planners.

[12] The reclassification from Order XXIV may well have caused the negative residual in section (a) of the table and inflated the positive residual in section (b).

to favour the latter. This section continues to analyse the repercussions of the changing industrial structure, as measured in the unemployment statistics of the period. This approach permits a rough analysis to be made of the state of the local labour market; analysis of past unemployment trends will show if any significant surplus or deficit of labour existed in the area.

Over the period, the rate of unemployment in the Study Area varied between 1·6% and 3·7%, with an average rate of 2·3%; this compared to the Scottish range of 2·5% to 5·4% an average of 3·6%.[13] At all times the rate of unemployment in the Study Area lay well below the Scottish figures, being typically about two-thirds of the national rate. In both cases, the pattern of unemployment showed a steady rise from the beginning of the period to a peak in the first quarter of 1963, then declined to 1966, with minor peaks in the third quarter of 1964 and 1965 and a rising trend towards the end of 1966. The behaviour of the rates would seem to indicate that the level of about 2% was the equilibrium rate; disturbances from this were quickly followed by adjustments back towards this level. As such, the Study Area was obviously one of the more prosperous regions in Scotland, although the improvements in the industrial structure of the latter helped to narrow the gap a little over the period.

The number of unemployed persons in the Study Area varied from about 700 in early 1966 to under 1,700 at the 1963 peak; between three-fifths and four-fifths of the total were males.[14] The peak of male unemployment of about 1,300 in 1963 was caused by a combination of mining closures culminating with Glenochil, the effect of a severe winter on the construction industry and extensive short-time working in the paper industry.[15] The recovery reflected more normal conditions in construction and paper and the emigration of many of the younger miners from the area.[16] The only other notable peak in male unemployment, in late 1965, while it coincided with the mild Scottish downturn, was exaggerated by an industrial dispute and strike of mining maintenance workers, with the lay-off of the other workers under safety legislation. Finally, the rising trend to the end of 1966 reflected partly the national slowdown, but also was inflated by the effects of another severe winter on construction.

On the other hand, the volatility of female unemployment over the period can be traced almost entirely to the Textile industry. All that can be added here is that the peaks in 1963, 1964 and 1966 all reflected short-time working rather than full unemployment, although the latter peak did contain some

[13] See figure 3.1. [14] See figure 3.2.

[15] Short-time working, where it involves any days of no employment during a working week, is designated 'temporarily stopped' by the D.E.P. and included in the unemployment statistics, although it is not unemployment in the normal sense of the word.

[16] The minutes of the D.E.P. quarterly meeting for October 1963 indicate that 75% of the unemployed males were unskilled and typically the older men left after emigration had taken place.

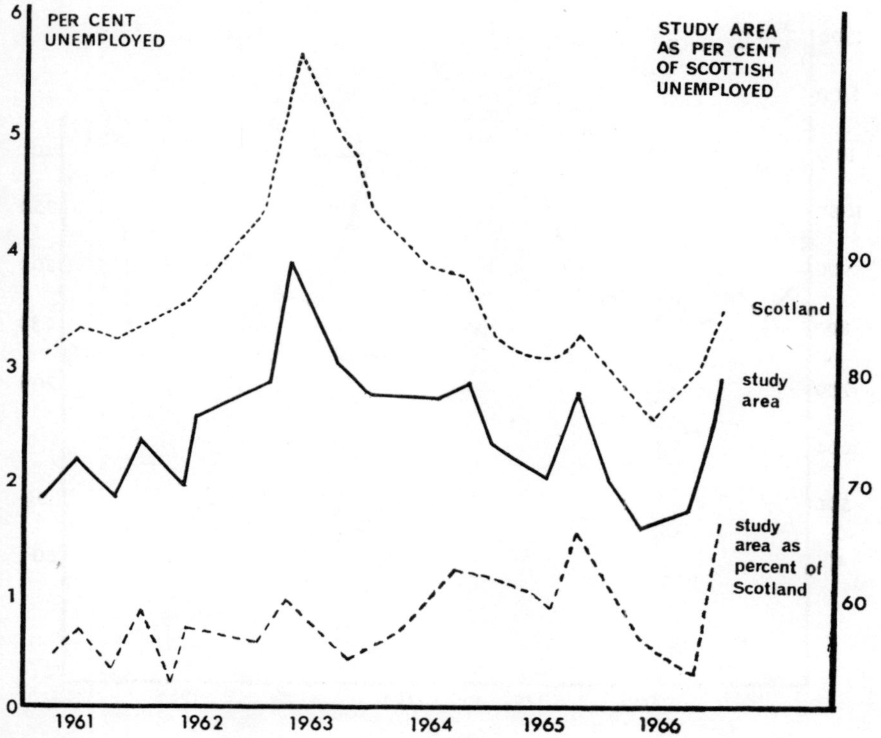

Figure 3.1

Percentage Unemployed, Scotland and Study Area, 1961–66 Seasonally Adjusted

genuine unemployment following closures of some smaller textile firms in the area.

The implication of these figures is that the peaks of male or female unemployment did not indicate any real or lasting surplus of labour supply over labour demand. They were either caused by short-time working, or unique local disturbances. While the national cycle undoubtedly exerted some pressure on the local labour market, this constituted only a minor element in unemployment. Relative to the Scottish pattern, the unemployment figures indicate that the Study Area had little to offer in the way of labour reserves by 1966.

This observation is confirmed by an analysis of the duration of unemployment.[17] For males, apart from the initial year of the period, the largest

[17] Data taken from the local office returns on unemployment. It must be remembered that the return does not state the actual duration of unemployment. It merely shows that, at end June each year, this was the analysis of the unemployed on the register. Since there is no sign of any cumulative build-up in the other columns, it suggests a quick turnover.

Figure 3.2

Persons Unemployed in the Study Area, 1961–66 (Seasonally Adjusted)

proportion of unemployment was relatively short-term in nature; over half the male unemployed have been quickly reabsorbed in the Study Area or surrounding districts. Long-term unemployed were typically about one-third of the total, with a hard core element of about 150 persons. Medium-term unemployment, very much the cyclical buffer, was virtually eliminated from 1964 onwards.

The pattern of female unemployment was broadly similar with, as one would expect, the long-term element of less importance than for males. With the medium-term component squeezed even more drastically than for males, by far the largest component of female unemployment has been of a short-term nature. As a final check on this, since the female labour market only covers females registered as prepared to work, an estimate was made of the Female Activity Rate[18] for the area. While the Scottish female activity rate for 1966 was 40·3%,[19] the Study Area rate was 41–44%. Almost certainly, a

[18] The Activity Rate is the economically active female labour force expressed as a percentage of female population 15 and over. The figures were taken from the Sample Census and are at 95% level of confidence.

[19] Digest of Scottish Statistics, No. 30, October 1967, table 42.

significantly higher proportion of the female population in the Study Area were economically active than was the case for Scotland as a whole; indeed, the rates indicate comparability with Glasgow and West Central and Tayside[20] which had the highest activity rates in Scotland for that year. At first sight, this confirms that there was little in the way of female labour reserves in the area, making a constraint for future internal and University growth. However, while there is a constraint, it is not likely to be a fixed one; it is expected that the national level of female activity rate will rise in the future, which will be reflected in the Study Area, as the non-operative type of work expands. This will be augmented by the inflow of immigrants to the area as the University expansion takes place which, in turn, will increase the local female population and therefore labour force.

In conclusion, the chapter has indicated that, over the period 1961–66 there took place a considerable swing towards employment in the Services sector, which had some effect on the relative importance of the various industries – more in terms of employment than income, owing to the male/female proportions of the industries affected. The type of growth in non-traditional industries caused a decline in the number of male jobs and an expansion in females employed. These changes appear to have had little effect on male unemployment locally, as a result of emigration and a switch to commuting to outside the area. On the other hand, the growth in female employment placed considerable pressure on labour reserves, although, in female employment, reserves are normally greater than indicated by employment figures. Nevertheless, the indications were that any further expansion in the area would place real pressure on local recruitment, wages and conditions of work.

[20] See The Intermediate Areas, 1969, CMND 3998, Appendix C, p. 214.

Table 3.1 *Distribution of Employment*

	1961				1966				
S.I.C. Order	*Study Area No.*	*%*	*Scotland %*	*Location Factor*	*Study Area No.*	*%*	*Scotland %*	*Location Factor*	*Study Area Change 1961–66 No.*
1. Agriculture	678	1·8	4·5	0·40	528	1·4	3·5	0·40	−150
2. Mining	5,113	13·8	4·2	3·29	3,350	8·9	2·7	3·30	−1,763
3. Food, Drink and Tobacco	2,339	6·3	4·6	1·37	3,075	5·5	4·6	1·20	−264
4. Chemicals	41	0·1	1·7	0·06	17	0·0	1·6	0·00	−24
5. Metal Manufacturing	13	0·0	2·7	0·00	47	0·1	2·4	0·04	+34
6. Engineering and Electrical	1,447	3·9	7·8	0·50	1,536	4·1	8·5	0·48	+89
7. Shipbuilding	17	0·0	3·0	0·00	17	0·0	2·2	0·00	0
8. Vehicles	89	0·2	1·7	0·11	14	0·0	2·0	0·00	−75
9. Metal goods	1,109	3·0	1·3	2·31	1,246	3·3	1·3	2·54	+137
10. Textiles	4,336	11·7	4·9	2·39	4,197	11·2	4·6	2·43	−139
11. Leather	81	0·2	0·2	1·00	7	0·0	0·2	0·00	−74
12. Clothing and Footwear	55	0·1	1·4	0·07	54	0·1	1·5	0·07	−1
13. Bricks etc.	1,364	3·7	1·0	3·70	1,667	4·4	1·1	4·00	+303
14. Timber etc.	396	1·1	1·1	1·00	379	1·0	1·1	0·91	+17
15. Paper and Printing	1,603	4·3	2·7	1·59	1,637	4·4	2·7	1·63	+34
16. Other manufacturing	235	0·6	0·9	0·67	236	0·6	0·8	0·75	+1
17. Construction	2,897	7·8	8·0	0·98	3,345	8·9	9·1	0·98	+448
18. Gas, Electricity	852	2·3	1·4	1·64	1,244	3·3	1·6	2·06	+392
19. Transport	1,734	4·7	8·4	0·56	1,677	4·5	7·3	0·62	+57
20. Distribution	3,513	9·5	13·3	0·71	3,657	9·8	13·4	0·73	+144
21. Insurance	509	1·4	1·9	0·74	767	2·0	2·1	0·95	+258
22. Professional Services	2,975	8·0	10·3	0·78	4,099	10·9	12·0	0·91	+1,124
23. Miscellaneous Services	3,102	8·4	7·7	1·09	3,689	9·8	8·5	1·15	+587
24. Public Administration	2,563	6·9	5·0	1·38	2,013	5·4	5·3	1·02	−550
	37,061				37,498				+437

Table 3.2 *Employment Changes in Study Area 1961–66 – National and Local Components*

C

	Study Area 1961 (*a*)	*Scotland* %Δ *1961–66* (*b*)	*Study Area adjusted by Scottish Rate* (*c*)	*Actual S.A. figures 1966* (*d*)	*Residual Study Area* (*d* – *c*) (*e*)	*L.F. of Study Area 1961*
1. Agriculture	678	−22·4	526	528	+2	0·40
2. Mining and Quarrying	5,113	−34·4	3,354	3,350	−4	3·29
3. Food, Drink and Tobacco	2,339	+3·0	2,409	2,075	−334	1·37
4. Chemicals	41	−8·7	37	17	−20	0·06
5. Metal Manufacturing	13	−9·6	12	47	+35	0·00
6. Engineering and Electrical	1,447	+10·0	1,592	1,536	−56	0·50
7. Shipbuilding	17	−24·6	13	17	+4	0·00
8. Vehicles	89	+16·6	104	14	−90	0·11
9. Metal goods	1,109	0·0	1,109	1,246	+137	2·31
10. Textiles	4,336	−5·4	4,102	4,197	+95	2·39
11. Leather	81	−9·5	73	7	−66	1·00
12. Clothing and Footwear	55	+5·0	58	54	−4	0·07
13. Bricks etc.	1,364	+3·5	1,412	1,667	+255	3·70
14. Timber etc.	396	−3·3	382	379	−3	1·00
15. Paper and Printing	1,603	+1·6	1,629	1,637	+8	1·59
16. Other manufacturing	235	−1·1	232	236	+4	0·67
17. Construction	2,897	+14·6	3,320	3,345	+25	0·98
18. Gas, Electricity and Water	852	+13·4	966	1,244	+278	1·64
19. Transport	1,734	−11·1	1,542	1,677	+135	0·56
20. Distribution	3,513	+2·0	3,583	3,657	+74	0·71
21. Insurance	509	+11·3	567	767	+200	0·74
22. Professional Services	2,975	+18·6	3,528	4,099	+571	0·78
23. Miscellaneous Services	3,102	+11·5	3,459	3,689	+230	1·09
24. Public Administration	2,563	+7·6	2,758	2,013	−745	1·38
	37,061		36,767	37,498	+731	

4

Projection of the Study Area's Population

Knowledge of present and recent population characteristics is not, of itself, sufficient. In the setting of planning targets and the process by which these are to be reached, it is essential to have some knowledge of future changes in both the total size and the age composition of the local population, particularly where it is reasonable to expect that these changes will be major rather than marginal. The link between total population size and spatial planning is obvious. Less obvious, but equally important, is the link between age composition and spatial planning, since each age group, young or elderly, has its own unique needs. Depending upon information on age structure as well as total size, plans can be laid for the provision of the necessary number and types of housing, its zoning, the allocation of space for education, medical, social amenity and recreational facilities.

The problem of future population needs is particularly acute where there is some evidence that strong internal growth forces exist already in the area and that the future development of the new industry is likely to draw a further inflow of population to the area. Population projections of some sort are obviously needed in this situation, in view of the possible extent of the changes involved even in the fairly medium term future.

One issue which must be recognised at the earliest stage is that internal and external growth forces may well conflict. It is at least possible that the additional employment offered by the new industry to the region, both directly and in the secondary growth which can be reasonably expected to follow, might well deplete the local labour reserves to such an extent that internal growth is seriously inhibited. Further, knowledge of the tight labour market conditions in the area could possibly divert potential new entrant firms to other areas, disturbing past or anticipated future patterns of migration. Each new project and its receiving region is likely to be unique in respect of their joint demands for internal labour and other facilities. In some cases, there will be conflict, the repercussions of which must be allowed for in the projection of population. The modifications, if any, required to the projection model and its inputs as a result of conflicting growth, must be a matter of judgement in each case.

For the Stirling Study Area, it would seem that there is no significant conflict between internal and external growth forces. While strong internal growth forces have been identified in earlier chapters, the employment demands from the University are, in many cases, for skills not normally available locally, so that much of the new labour force will be brought to or attracted into the area from outside its boundaries. There is a heavy to total reliance on immigrants for academic, technical and senior administration posts. Only in the University's demand for more junior non-academic staff is any real pressure placed on the local labour market. So far, possibly due to the availability of dependents of the various types of immigrants to the area, there is no evidence of any real constraint having been imposed on local industrial growth. Apparently, too, for new firms considering the area, the existence of the University has proved to be an attraction rather than the opposite. It would seem from current evidence that no major conflict is likely in the near future.

The approach followed in the Stirling case study was to move towards the objective of providing estimates of future local population and employment in two stages. Firstly, estimates were made of population and employment totals attributable to purely internal forces, i.e. independent of any influence from University growth and secondary developments around this. This chapter covers the internal projections for local population; the projection of employment is discussed in Chapter 5. Secondly, the population and employment totals attributable to the University and its secondary growth, were estimated for the same target years; the University's impact on employment is covered in Chapter 7, and on population in Chapter 8. Finally, in Chapter 9, the two sources of growth are drawn together and the overall situation examined.

The Population Projection Model

The first step in making population projections is to determine the base date from which the projection is made, and the target dates to which it has to be taken. Given the age and sex detail needed for a projection model, the base date must be a full Census year when, for most Local Authority regions a full breakdown of population by sex and 5-year age groups is normally possible. In setting the target dates to which the projection will be taken, it must be remembered that, inevitably, the longer a projection continues the more inaccurate it must become. This follows from the fact that any projection model must be based on the assumption of a fair number of very rigid relationships, and it is unlikely that the patterns assumed to remain constant will continue to hold true over a prolonged period. Indeed, it is normal to allow for this by making a series of projections based on slightly different values for the basic components of the model, so that the final estimates take the form of a population range within which, given some inevitable changes in the relationships over the period, the actual population can be expected to lie.

For the Stirling case study, the base year was taken as 1961 rather than 1966, to gain access to the full Census return, although the Sample Census of the latter date coincided more neatly with the start of work on the University.[1] The target years for the projection were taken as 1976 and 1981, since these years represented convenient stages in the planned growth of the new University.[2]

The next step, having determined the period of the projection, is to decide on the type of projection model to be used.[3] It is argued here that, in most cases, there is no real need to develop and use any of the more sophisticated types of population projection models unless these satisfy the highly specific information needs of the planners. The reasons for this are that, firstly, much of the data required by such models, e.g. fertility rates, or data on the duration of marriage, is not available at sub-regional level, and secondly, again at sub-regional level, some of the variables excluded (e.g. availability and cost of housing), are likely to be of more importance than some of the variables included (e.g. probability of divorce or widowhood and re-marriage fertility rates). Any model must be a simplification of the complex relationships of reality and the simplified type of projection model used here is no less defensible for reason of its simplicity; care has been taken to base it on what are conventionally regarded as the main variables and relationships.

The model[4] uses four sources of information. Firstly, the base population, classified by 5-year age group and sex, was taken from the Census report of 1961. This base population was then adjusted over the projection period for births, deaths and migration. The data for births[5] was calculated from age specific fertility rates based on the average Scottish figures, adjusted to predict total births per annum for the Study Area. Similarly, the data for deaths[5] was calculated from age specific mortality rates, based on average Scottish figures, and adjusted to predict annual deaths in the Study Area. Finally, the migration figures and age structure used were based on the assumptions discussed below.

Since population projections are based on fairly rigorous conditions and formalised relationships, it is normal to make a series of projections, in which

[1] However, the projected figures for 1966 were compared to the broader results of the Sample Census published and unpublished returns to check that the model was functioning accurately over this early period.

[2] See Chapter 7 for a brief account of the University's Development Plan.

[3] A discussion of the various types of model can be found in publications such as *Demography*, 3rd edition, P. R. Cox, 1966. A more illustrative discussion of projection methods is contained in *Demographic Analysis*, chapter 9, B. Benjamin, 1968. Finally, an excellent discussion of methods and problems likely to be encountered in projections is contained in *The Study of Population*, edited by P. M. Hauser and O. D. Duncan, chapter 23 by J. V. Grauman.

[4] See Appendix A to this chapter.

[5] See Appendix B to this Chapter.

some basic condition is allowed to vary and the effect of these variations observed. If the direction and volume of the Study Area's migration flow seems likely to remain constant for the future, the series of projections can be made incorporating combinations of rising and falling rates for births and deaths over the period to produce a 'band' within which total population might fall in the future. Alternatively, if it is felt that the direction and/or volume of the net migration flow is likely to vary significantly over the period from its previous pattern, then the birth rate and death rate inputs used can be set at some average projected level for the period ahead, and the migration input allowed to fluctuate and set the projected population range.[6]

For the Stirling Study Area, this latter approach was taken. Analysis of past migration flows had indicated that, while the direction of net migration was a net outflow over the period, the rate of loss had fallen from an average of 270 persons per annum for 1951–61 to about 180 persons per annum for 1961–66, at a time when the Scottish rate was rising markedly. Indeed, for the later period, many sections of the Study Area showed significant net inflows, with only the urban centres reflecting the Scottish pattern. It was felt that there were two main reasons why the net migration loss from the Study Area overall might well decline, or be replaced by a net gain over the period of the projection. Firstly, the Registrar-General has forecast[7] that the rate of migration loss from Scotland will fall over the period to a lower level than has been experienced since 1951; if this is reflected in the urban sections of the Stirling Study Area, then the continuing expansion from the other sections could well result in a migration flow balance, or even net gain. Secondly, current road developments from the Study Area to the rest of the Central belt and the North, taken with the apparently growing willingness to commute greater distances to Glasgow and Edinburgh, as well as the Falkirk/Grangemouth complex, could result in considerable residential expansion in the area.

On the grounds that possible changes in the direction and volume of the migration flow are likely to be more significant than any changes in birth and death rates over the projection period, the former has been chosen as the condition allowed to vary in the projections made. Three projections have been made on the basis of constant birth and mortality rates over the period to 1981. Projection 1, the lower case, assumes a continuing net loss of 300 persons per annum, i.e. roughly of the same magnitude as experienced over the 1950's; it is unlikely that net migration loss in the future will be above this level. Projection 2, on the other hand, assumes that migration flows will balance throughout the period, i.e. zero net migration. Finally, Projection 3 assumes that there will be a net migration gain annually of 300 persons for

[6] Sensitivity tests in the Stirling case study indicated that results would be affected more by variation in migration than in birth rates and death rates, for the period chosen.

[7] *Annual Report of Registrar-General for Scotland*, 1967, p. 88.

the duration of the period; within the conditions specified for birth and death rates, it takes the nature of an upper case.

The basic formula used[8] for the projections can be taken most easily from Projection II, where there is no emigration. Here each 5-year age group (P_x) is projected over the quinquennium (i.e. from year $n+1$ to $n+6$) on the basis of the numbers who survive the period, i.e.

$$^{n+6}P_{x+5} = {}^{n+1}P_x \,.\, {}^{5}\Pi_x \tag{1}$$

where ${}^{5}\Pi_x$ represents the survival factor for that age group over the quinquennium. In Projection I, where there is a net migration outflow for each year of the period, then for any age group, migrants (M_x) for the period must be deducted from the survivors, i.e.

$$^{n+6}P_{x+5} = {}^{n+1}P_x \,.\, {}^{5}\Pi_x - \sum_{r=1}^{5} ({}^{n+r}M_x) \tag{2}$$

Finally, in the case of Projection III, where there is a net migration inflow over the period, the migrants to the age group must be added to the survivors,[9] i.e.

$$^{n+6}P_{x+5} = {}^{n+1}P_x \,.\, {}^{5}\Pi_x + \sum_{r=1}^{5} ({}^{n+r}M_x) \tag{3}$$

This basic formula cannot, however, be used for all the age groups in the population. In particular, adjustments must be made for the ageing process of the 0–4 age group, to allow for the marked differences in mortality rates experienced over this age range. Mortality rates also pose a problem for the ageing of the 80 and over age groups and again the basic formula must be modified to take account of this. Finally, the projection of a 0–4 age group at the end of the period involves the computation of births over the period, adjusted for deaths and migration. All of these modifications are discussed in Appendix A to this Chapter.

Population Projections for the Stirling Study Area

Using the model developed above, population projections were made to show the consequences of purely internal growth, i.e. growth uninfluenced by University forces. The projections indicate[10] that, with a net outward flow of about 300 persons per annum, the population of the Study Area would increase from its base of 92,900 in 1961 to about 100,900 by 1976 (an increase of 8·6% or about 8,000 persons) and about 103,300 by 1981 (11·2% or 10,400 persons). For Projection II, with its zero migration flow, there would be an

[8] See Appendix A for the full discussion of the model's system of equations for the various age groups and births.

[9] See Appendix A for a discussion of the survival of migrants over the period and the justification for assuming zero deaths, as in equation (3) above.

[10] See Tables 4.1, 4.2 and 4.3, pages 32 and 33.

increase to about 106,400 by 1976 (14·6% or about 13,500 persons), and about 111,000 (19·5% or 18,100) by 1981. Finally, for Projection III, with its net migration inflow of 300 persons per annum, there would be an increase to about 111,800 by 1976 (20·3% or 18,900 persons) and about 118,500 by 1981 (an overall increase of 27·5% or 25,600 persons). These figures indicate a population band of between 101,000 to 112,000 for 1976, and 103,000 to 118,000 for 1981.

Projection II, with a zero migration flow, effectively estimates the natural increase of the population of the Study Area over the period. Comparison with Projection I shows that even a relatively mild migration loss of 300 persons per annum causes a shortfall of 7,700 persons over a twenty-year period – 1,700 more than the loss of the actual migrants, due to the loss of their potential children over the period.[11] On the other hand, comparison of Projections II and III shows the result of an annual gain of 300 persons, with a surplus of about 7,500 over the natural increase, again 1,500 more than the actual migrants gained. The comparison of Projections I and III provides a fairly clear indication of the extent to which the more fortunate 'migration gain' areas of Scotland experience an explosive rate of population growth relative to the other areas, since they do not only retain their own natural increase but also receive a further transfusion of, typically, a younger and more active population.

The effects of migration patterns can be seen very clearly from an analysis of the relative rates of growth. Not only does Projection I have a relatively slower rate of growth than Projection II, and this in turn relatively slower than Projection III, but there is a significant cumulative effect. Owing to the drain of net migration loss from reproductive groups, a population will increase at a more and more sluggish rate, relative to its rate of natural increase; conversely, a population with a net migration gain will tend to grow at an increasing rate. Thus the gap made by different patterns will widen at an increasing rate over time.

If the effects of migration patterns are applied to the age structure of the population, then over the period to 1976 there would be a natural increase of about 3,200 persons in the age group 0–14. On the other hand, the Projection I conditions of net migration loss would cause a shortfall of 1,500 from this figure, i.e. a loss of almost half the natural increase. Under the Projection III conditions, the natural increase in this age group would be exceeded by a further 1,400. A similar pattern emerges for the other age groups, with the impact of migration declining in the higher age groups, partly since these are not normally affected much by migration and partly because the heavier

[11] Most estimated age structures of migrants indicate that there is a heavy concentration on the 20–39 age range, the key reproductive groups in the community. Therefore loss or gain of migrants involves the secondary loss or gain of both actual and potential child dependants. See also later comments in Chapters 9 and 10.

mortality rates tend to even out any differences which do occur. For the 15–39 age group, there would be a natural increase of about 6,900 persons from the base population, with Projection I losing and Projection III gaining about one-third of this. For the 40–64 age group, the natural increase of Projection II shows only 300 persons more than for the base year, due in part to the movement of depleted (by emigration in earlier years) younger age groups into this section and, in part, the assumption of a zero migration flow here; Projection I conditions indicate a loss of about 1,400 persons in this age group from the base year total and Projection III a gain of about 2,000. The final age group for '65 and over' in common with the projections of the Registrar-General and others, increases markedly both in absolute numbers and in relative size under all projection conditions, to contain about 3,000 persons more than in 1961.

Examination of the projection figures for 1981 offers no contradiction to the findings for 1976. They show that further natural increases of about 1,000 in age group 0–14, 3,000 in age group 15–39, about 600 in age group 65 and over and a loss of about 500 in age group 40–64, have been estimated. Projection I conditions cause a more sluggish rise in all groups, increasing over the period 1976–81 by 2,500 persons, or 2·3% compared with the increase overall of 4,600 or 4·3% for Projection II and 6,700 or 6% for Projection III.

The final result, in all cases, is that the assumptions made on the nature of the age structure of the migration flows causes a transition to a relatively younger population than the base year, this bias towards the younger age groups being accelerated towards the end of the period in the zero migration or net migration inflow figures.

Table 4.1

Projected Total Population of the Study Area

	Projection I	*Projection II*	*Projection III*
1961	92,905	92,905	92,905
1966	95,755	97,372	98,973
1971	98,467	101,927	105,327
1976	100,911	106,395	111,770
1981	103,330	110,984	118,485

Table 4.2
Age Structure of Projected Population (1976)

All Persons 1961 and 1976

	1961		*1976*					
Age	*Persons*	%	*I*	%	*II*	%	*III*	%
0–14	25,445	27·4	27,152	26·9	28,654	26·9	30,051	26·9
15–39	30,614	33·0	35,358	35·0	37,538	35·3	39,722	35·5
40–64	27,603	29·7	26,240	26·0	27,934	26·3	29,623	26·5
65 and over	9,243	9·9	12,161	12·1	12,269	11·5	12,374	11·1
	92,905		100,911		106,395		111,770	

Table 4.3
Age Structure of Projected Population (1981)

	1961		*1981*					
Age	*Persons*	%	*I*	%	*II*	%	*III*	%
0–14	25,445	27·4	27,636	26·7	29,797	26·8	31,825	26·9
15–39	30,614	33·0	38,133	36·9	40,877	36·8	43,608	36·8
40–64	27,603	29·7	24,859	24·1	27,403	24·7	29,941	25·3
65 and over	9,243	9·9	12,702	12·3	12,907	11·6	13,111	11·1
	92,905		103,330		110,984		118,485	

APPENDIX A

The Population Projection Model

Taking the 1961 Census population, adjusted to bring it to 30th June 1961, as its base population, the model projects the 5-year age groups over a series of quinquennial steps from 1961 to 1981; this base population is subject to the three main adjustments of deaths, births and migration.

(*a*) *Deaths*

The probability of death in any year for a person in the 5-year age group x is given by the value of q_x. The probability of survival, or simply the survival factor is therefore $\pi_x = 1 - q_x$. Since the probability of death over a quinquennium for a given age group will be five times the probability of death in one year, or $5q_x$, then the survival factor over the five years is

$$^5\pi_x = 1 - 5q_x \qquad (1)$$

Thus, where there is no net migration flow to be taken into account, the numbers of the population of age group $x(P_x)$ surviving the quinquennium can be calculated as $P_x \,.\, {}^5\pi_x$.

Use is made of two types of modified survival factors. In the case of the final two age groups for '80–4' and '85 and over', adjustment for death via a straightforward survival factor of $^5\pi_x$ (i.e. $1 - 5q_x$) results in too severe a reduction of population of this age. Here the device of applying q_x to survivors of successive years has been used, i.e. a one-year survival factor of π_x is applied to the survivors of the first year of the quinquennium, namely, $P_x\pi_x$, as $(P_x\pi_x)\pi_x$, and becomes $P_x(\pi_x)^2$; thus the modified survival factor for these age groups for the quinquennium becomes $P_x(\pi_x)^5$. The second type of modification used is where births, or in-migrants, are under consideration; both of these sources of population must be treated not only as annual flows during each quinquennium but also as flows during or within each year itself. This implies that for, say, immigrants, the total coming into the Study Area in year one of the period are exposed, on average, to only half of the probability of death for that year (i.e. some of the migrants arrive at the beginning, some in the middle and some at the end of the period, each with a different time of exposure to death – so that only the first migrants are exposed to the full q_x). Thus, for those exposed to only half the annual probability of death, a separate survival factor of $\pi'_x = 1 - \frac{1}{2}q_x$ is calculated and applied; for simplicity, it is assumed that, for the remainder of the quinquennium following their first year of entry, survivors are exposed to the full probability of death for each year, so that the full adjustment for first year of the quinquennium entrants becomes, for immigrants, $M_x \,.\, \pi'_x \,.\, {}^4\pi_x$. (For second year entrants it would become $M_x \,.\, \pi'_x \,.\, {}^3\pi_x$ and so on.) The same type of survival factor is used for births, i.e. a double adjustment for survival of first then subsequent years of life during the quinquennium in question.

(*b*) *Births*

Total births for any single year of the projection period can be estimated by applying the total fertility rate[1] to all women of reproductive age alive in that year, i.e. $F_t \,.\, P_y$. When estimating births over a quinquennium, however, given no migration net flow[2] to complicate the issue, P_y will decline under the incidence of death, as it affects each age group within the range 15–49 years.

[1] See Appendix B.

[2] For correction of formula for migration effect, see later section (*c*) of this Appendix.

The survivors of the original group of women of reproductive age, P_y becomes $P_y{}^5\pi_y$ (where ${}^5\pi_y$ is merely a summary expression for all the quinquennial survival factors for each age group of this section of the population). As a result of this, given a constant fertility rate F_t, total births will fall in successive years as the quinquennium progresses. To simplify, it has been assumed that there is a constant annual flow of births (B_0), which is made up of half the births from women alive at the beginning of the period $(n+1)$ and half the births from women alive at the end of the quinquennium $(n+6)$, i.e.

$$B_0 = \frac{F_t({}^{n+1}P_y + {}^{n+6}P_y \,.\, {}^5\pi_y)}{2} \tag{2}$$

(*c*) *Migration*

The Registrar-General's estimates of net migration flow for Scotland allow the calculation of the number of persons, male and female of the net flow of the Study Area for any year, or over the quinquennium. Net migrants for any single year are denoted by the symbol M_x, where x is again the 5-year age group of the migrant.

For Projection I, it is assumed that there is a net annual outflow of 300 persons from the Study Area. For the purposes of the projection formulae, it is also assumed that this figure for emigration, when taken over the quinquennium (giving a total of 1,500 emigrants), is net of death. The emigration total represents those who have actually left the Study Area, not merely those intending to emigrate (some of whom are likely to have died over the quinquennium). Thus, in Projection I, the emigration adjustment is:

$$-\sum_{r=1}^{5} {}^{n+r}M_x \tag{3}$$

For Projection III, it is assumed that there is a net inflow of migrants to the Study Area of 300 persons per annum. In this case, however, the inflow enters the Study Area during each year of the quinquennium, thus experiencing a modified probability of death. Thus a dual survival factor must be used, with its first component relating to the year of entry into the Study Area and its second component relating to subsequent years of the quinquennium, when, for simplicity, it is assumed that immigrants face the full annual probability of death. For this projection, the formula adjustment for immigration becomes:

$$+\sum_{r=1}^{5} {}^{n+r}M_x \,.\, \pi'_x \, {}^{5-r}\pi_x \tag{4}$$

However, in the actual computation of the projection by quinquennium, the fairly complex survival adjustments for immigrants have an insignificant effect on the migration figure for most age groups; if migration inflow over the quinquennium into any given age group (apart from 'under 1') is taken as net of death, in no case is there a difference of more than one person per age group per quinquennium. The reasons for this are fairly obvious, given the age structure of the migration flow. Migration is at its heaviest in younger age groups, where q_x is at an extremely low value, so that ignoring the latter entirely, including its modified first year, has little effect on the M_x total. Equally, where q_x rises to a more significant level, i.e. in the older age groups, migration flow is either a trickle, or even zero, over the quinquennium; again the effect on M_x is negligible. Thus, for all practical purposes, the net inflow, as with the net outflow, can be taken as net of death and the formula simplified to:

$$+\sum_{r=1}^{5} {}^{n+r}M_x \qquad (4')$$

Finally, the formulae for estimating births can be adjusted to take account of migration effects. Projection II, with zero net migration remains as in section (*b*) of this Appendix. Projection I, with new outflow becomes:

$$B_0 = \frac{F_t[{}^{n+1}P_y + ({}^{n+1}P_y \,.\, {}^{5}\pi_y - \sum_{r=1}^{5} {}^{n+r}M_y)]}{2} \qquad (2')$$

Projection III, with a net migration inflow, becomes:

$$B_0 = \frac{F_t[{}^{n+1}P_y + ({}^{n+1}P_y \,.\, {}^{5}\pi_y + \sum_{r=1}^{5} {}^{n+r}M_y)]}{2} \qquad (2'')$$

(*d*) *The final projection formulae*

The model projects the male and female population by 5-year age group in quinquennial steps from 1961 ($n+1$) to 1981.

(i) For all age groups other than '0–4', '80–4' and '85 and over' in 1966 (year $n+6$), the projection formula for zero net migration (Projection II) is:

$$ {}^{n+6}P_{x+5} = {}^{n+1}P_x \, {}^{5}\pi_x \qquad (5)$$

For Projection I the formula is:

$$ {}^{n+6}P_{x+5} = {}^{n+1}P_x \,.\, {}^{5}\pi_x - \sum_{r=1}^{5} {}^{n+r}M_x \qquad (5')$$

For Projection III the formula is:

$$ {}^{n+6}P_{x+5} = {}^{n+1}P_x \, {}^{5}\pi_x + \sum_{r=1}^{5} {}^{n+r}M_x \qquad (5'')$$

(ii) In projecting for age group '0–4', account must be taken of the variation in death rates between the first year of life and the remainder of the age range '1–4'. While several possible approaches exist, it was decided to calculate two separate survival factors, one for the first year of life (π_0) and one covering any year in the range 1–4 (π_α). Further, the first survival must be modified, as discussed previously, to π_0.
The formula for Projection II in this age group becomes:

$$^{n+6}P_{0-4} = \sum_{r=1}^{5} {}^{n+r}B_0 \,.\, \pi_0' \,.\, {}^{5-r}\pi_\alpha \tag{6}$$

For Projection I, the formula takes account of net emigration:

$$^{n+6}P_{0-4} = \sum_{r=1}^{5} {}^{n+r}B_0 \,.\, \pi_0' \,.\, {}^{5-r}\pi_\alpha - \sum_{r=1}^{5} {}^{n+r}M_0 \tag{6'}$$

For Projection III, the formula takes account of net immigration and is the only age group where the survival factor for migrants is modified as discussed previously (since both migration flow and q_x are significant here). It becomes:

$$^{n+6}P_{0-4} = \sum_{r=1}^{5} ({}^{n+r}B_0 + {}^{n+r}M_0) \,.\, \pi_0' \,.\, {}^{5-r}\pi_\alpha \tag{6''}$$

Formulae for age groups '80–4' and '85 and over'

The adjustment to the quinquennial survival factor has been discussed earlier and the modified survival factor is used for both age groups. For age group '80–4' the projection formula is:

$$^{n+6}P_{80-4} = {}^{n+1}P_{75-9}\,(\pi_{75-9})^5 \tag{7}$$

In the case of the older age group, '85 and over', there are two sources of population by year $n+6$, namely survivors over the quinquennium from age group '80–4' and survivors of the population aged '85 and over' of year $n+1$. Thus:

$$^{n+6}P_{85-} = {}^{n+1}P_{80-4}\,(\pi_{80-4})^5 + {}^{n+1}P_{85-}\,(\pi_{85-})^5 \tag{8}$$

In neither case are there any migration adjustments for inflow or outflow. The formulae are the same for Projections I, II and III.

The projected population totals for each quinquennium are given in Table (a) of this appendix. The 1976 projections by 5-year age group and sex are given in Tables (b) and (c) and, for 1981, Tables (d) and (e), on pages 38, 39 and 40.

Table (a) *Projected population totals for each quinquennium*

	1961	1966	1971	1976	1981
Projection I					
Males	44,682	46,193	47,661	48,998	50,324
Females	48,223	49,562	50,806	51,913	53,006
Total	92,905	95,755	98,467	100,911	103,330
Projection II					
Males	44,682	47,067	49,509	51,908	54,368
Females	48,223	50,305	52,418	54,487	56,616
Total	92,905	97,372	101,927	106,395	110,984
Projection III					
Males	44,682	47,920	51,313	54,752	58,321
Females	48,223	51,053	54,014	57,018	60,164
Total	92,905	98,973	105,327	111,770	118,485

Table (b) *Age Structure Comparison of Projections, 1976*

Male

	1961		*1976*					
Age	*Persons*	%	*I*	%	*II*	%	*III*	%
0–4	4,643	5·0	4,761	4·7	5,089	4·8	5,393	4·8
5–9	3,957	4·3	4,669	4·6	4,921	4·6	5,154	4·6
10–14	4,417	4·8	4,505	4·5	4,703	4·4	4,877	4·4
15–19	3,377	3·6	4,440	4·4	4,591	4·3	4,732	4·2
20–24	2,690	2·9	3,765	3·7	3,921	3·7	4,076	3·6
25–29	2,869	3·1	4,162	4·1	4,367	4·1	4,581	4·1
30–34	2,882	3·1	3,043	3·0	3,327	3·1	3,610	3·2
35–39	3,099	3·3	2,282	2·3	2,636	2·5	2,990	2·7
40–44	2,836	3·1	2,472	2·4	2,789	2·6	3,106	2·8
45–49	2,900	3·1	2,497	2·5	2,759	2·6	3,018	2·7
50–54	2,875	3·1	2,707	2·6	2,883	2·7	3,059	2·7
55–59	2,600	2·8	2,390	2·4	2,513	2·4	2,636	2·4
60–64	1,916	2·1	2,297	2·3	2,363	2·2	2,428	2·2
65–69	1,367	1·5	2,093	2·1	2,125	2·0	2,155	1·9
70–74	1,023	1·1	1,545	1·5	1,557	1·5	1,568	1·3
75–79	692	0·7	803	0·8	807	0·8	810	0·7
80–84	378	0·4	361	0·4	362	0·3	363	0·3
85 and over	161	0·2	195	0·2	195	0·2	196	0·2
	44,682		48,998		51,908		54,752	

Table (c) *Age Structure Comparison of Projections, 1976*

Female

	1961		1976					
Age	*Persons*	%	*I*	%	*II*	%	*III*	%
0–4	4,455	4·8	4,499	4·5	4,815	4·5	5,105	4·6
5–9	3,756	4·0	4,418	4·4	4,663	4·4	4,890	4·4
10–14	4,217	4·5	4,300	4·3	4,463	4·2	4,632	4·1
15–19	3,354	3·6	4,280	4·2	4,420	4·2	4,560	4·1
20–24	3,060	3·3	3,583	3·6	3,736	3·5	3,889	3·5
25–29	2,901	3·1	3,995	4·0	4,190	3·9	4,385	3·9
30–34	3,143	3·4	3,074	3·0	3,326	3·1	3,577	3·2
35–39	3,239	3·5	2,725	2·7	3,024	2·8	3,322	3·0
40–44	3,051	3·3	2,577	2·6	2,848	2·7	3,119	2·8
45–49	3,146	3·4	2,848	2·8	3,052	2·9	3,255	2·9
50–54	3,094	3·3	2,959	2·9	3,091	2·9	3,222	2·9
55–59	2,790	3·0	2,746	2·7	2,833	2·7	2,920	2·6
60–64	2,395	2·6	2,747	2·7	2,803	2·6	2,860	2·6
65–69	1,995	2·1	2,529	2·5	2,564	2·4	2,599	2·3
70–74	1,553	1·7	2,031	2·0	2,049	1·9	2,066	1·8
75–79	1,098	1·2	1,407	1·4	1,413	1·3	1,419	1·3
80–84	667	0·7	782	0·8	784	0·7	785	0·7
85–89	299	0·3	413	0·4	413	0·4	413	0·4
	48,223		51,913		54,487		57,018	

Table (d) *Age Structure Comparison of Projections, 1981*

Male

	1961		1981					
Age	*Persons*	%	*I*	%	*II*	%	*III*	%
0–4	4,643	5·0	4,900	4·7	5,333	4·8	5,742	4·8
5–9	3,957	4·3	4,694	4·5	5,060	4·6	5,402	4·6
10–14	4,417	4·8	4,604	4·5	4,906	4·4	5,189	4·4
15–19	3,377	3·6	4,442	4·3	4,691	4·2	4,915	4·1
20–24	2,690	2·9	4,379	4·2	4,574	4·1	4,769	4·0
25–29	2,869	3·1	3,634	3·5	3,901	3·5	4,166	3·5
30–34	2,882	3·1	4,016	3·9	4,339	3·9	4,672	3·9
35–39	3,099	3·3	2,890	2·8	3,298	3·0	3,704	3·1
40–44	2,836	3·1	2,177	2·1	2,602	2·3	3,026	2·6
45–49	2,900	3·1	2,352	2·3	2,728	2·5	3,104	2·6
50–54	2,875	3·1	2,364	2·3	2,659	2·4	2,950	2·5
55–59	2,600	2·8	2,521	2·4	2,710	2·4	2,900	2·4
60–64	1,916	2·1	2,140	2·1	2,260	2·0	2,379	2·0
65–69	1,367	1·5	2,005	1·9	2,066	1·9	2,126	1·8
70–74	1,023	1·1	1,592	1·5	1,618	1·5	1,644	1·4
75–79	692	0·7	977	0·9	984	0·9	991	0·8
80–84	378	0·4	441	0·4	443	0·4	445	0·4
85 and over	196	0·2	196	0·2	196	0·2	197	0·2
	44 682		50,324		54,368		58,321	

Table (e) *Age Structure Comparison of Projections, 1981*

Female

	1961		*1981*					
Age	*Persons*	%	*I*	%	*II*	%	*III*	%
0–4	4,455	4·8	4,638	4·6	5,050	4·6	5,440	4·6
5–9	3,756	4·0	4,440	4·3	4,792	4·3	5,119	4·3
10–14	4,217	4·5	4,360	4·2	4,656	4·2	4,933	4·2
15–19	3,354	3·6	4,242	4·1	4,456	4·0	4,676	4·0
20–24	3,060	3·3	4,220	4·1	4,411	4·0	4,601	3·9
25–29	2,901	3·1	3,481	3·4	3,726	3·4	3,972	3·4
30–34	3,143	3·4	3,872	3·7	4,174	3·8	4,477	3·8
35–39	3,239	3·5	2,957	2·9	3,307	3·0	3,656	3·1
40–44	3,051	3·3	2,635	2·6	2,997	2·7	3,358	2·8
45–49	3,146	3·4	2,497	2·4	2,806	2·5	3,115	2·6
50–54	3,094	3·3	2,756	2·7	2,982	2·7	3,207	2·7
55–59	2,790	3·0	2,833	2·7	2,981	2·7	3,129	2·6
60–64	2,395	2·6	2,584	2·5	2,678	2·4	2,773	2·3
65–69	1,995	2·1	2,491	2·4	2,548	2·3	2,606	2·2
70–74	1,553	1·7	2,158	2·1	2,191	2·0	2,224	1·9
75–79	1,098	1·2	1,543	1·5	1,557	1·4	1,570	1·3
80–84	677	0·7	851	0·8	855	0·8	858	0·7
85 and over	299	0·3	448	0·4	449	0·4	450	0·4
	48,223		53,006		56,616		60,164	

APPENDIX B

Fertility, Mortality and Migration Rates

(1) *Fertility rates for births projection*

In forecasting births, projection models of the component type, giving some weighting to variables such as proportion of women married, duration of marriage (since birth is likeliest in the earlier years of marriage), the likely incidence of divorce and widowhood over the period, with an adjustment for probability of remarriage during the period and probable trends in illegitimate births. Because of the difficulties involved in collecting and using at sub-regional level much of the statistics concerned with these variables, I have simplified the relationship between women of fertile age and births. If it is assumed that, over the period 1961–81, there are no significant changes in the proportion of women married,[1] that the duration of marriage pattern

[1] Effectively the proportion chosen is not that ruling at the beginning of the period, but the average proportion for 1960–67.

remains constant, that, at sub-region level, divorce and widowhood with possible remarriage have an insignificant effect on births and resultant population, then a fertility rate can be calculated and applied to all women of reproductive age, married and unmarried (thus covering illegitimacy), to obtain a total of live births for any year.

At sub-regional level, however, the Registrar-General statistics provide no age breakdown of women giving birth. From the statistics for all Scotland[2] for the period 1960–67 inclusive, average age specific fertility rates for all women were calculated. These rates were then applied to female population in the Study Area aged 15–49 and total births calculated. Next, total births in the Study Area were averaged over the period and compared to the estimates; the age specific fertility rates were then adjusted in the light of their comparison and then converted to a total fertility rate (F_t), which, when applied to all women aged 15–49 (P_y) yielded the average annual total of births.[3]

(2) *Mortality rates and survival factors*

For the purposes of projection the incidence of death must be calculated not for total population, but by sex and age group. Again it is impossible to obtain all the necessary data by sex and age at sub-regional level to allow the calculation of local age specific mortality rates.[4] Once again the rates used had to be calculated from figures relating to the whole of Scotland.[5] Even here, age specific mortality rates for all age groups over 15 years of age, are given in 10-year age groups, with an open-ended age group for '85 and over'. For the purposes of the projection, it was necessary to estimate A.S.M.R. for 5-year age groups.

The method adopted was to plot the average Scottish A.S.M.R. for the period 1960-67 on semi-log graphs and fit curves by eye. The A.S.M.R. for male and female 5-year age groups were then estimated by interpolation. The resultant mortality rates were then applied to the base population to estimate a figure for total deaths per annum for the Study Area. An annual average of actual deaths for the period was then calculated[6] and compared to the estimates, with the age specific mortality rates then adjusted to predict actual deaths.

In any year, the population in age group x will either survive or die ($\pi_x + q_x = 1$), thus the survival factor[7] per thousand of population for any

[2] Annual Reports of the Registrar-General, table 23.

[3] See Table (a), page 42.

[4] The most detailed set of local statistics in the Reports (table 55) does not cover many parts of the Study Area. Other tables do not attempt a sex breakdown and, in any case, still omit Central D.C. No. 1.

[5] Annual Reports of Registrar-General, table T37, averaged 1960–67.

[6] Source data from Annual Reports, tables 7 and 7a.

[7] See discussion on calculation of quinquennial survival factors in Appendix A.

age group x, is $\pi_x = 1 - q_x$. The survival factors for the quinquennium are given in Table (b).

(3) *Migration: sex and age assumptions for the projection*

Several alternative sources of information were available from which assumptions on the Study Area's migration pattern over the projection period could have been made, such as New Town studies, Census (1961) Migration Tables, or Glasgow overspill statistics.

However, for a number of reasons, it was decided to use the unpublished net migration estimates of the Registrar-General for Scotland. Firstly, while their age and sex pattern is based on the sample surveys on migration in the Census Reports for 1961 and 1966, it has been broken down from the rather broad age groups of the Census to the 5-year age groups used for the rest of the projection. Secondly, the Registrar's office have further adjusted the Census figures in the light of results from their own series of samples for migration by air and sea and also in light of their experience or, for example, age errors in survey returns. Thirdly, the pattern is based on all Scotland, has been computed and checked annually, so far as is possible, has been used over a fair period of time and has tended to show a steady, confirmed (by their various surveys) pattern, uninfluenced by minor, sub-regional quirks.

The number of migrants by age group are shown on Table (c).

Table (a)

Age Specific and Total Fertility Rates for Study Area

Age	*1961 Females*	*Fertility rate (per '000)*
15–19	3,354	40·02
20–24	3,060	186·48
25–29	2,901	197·51
30–34	3,143	117·52
35–39	3,239	57·65
40–44	3,051	15·57
45–49	3,146	0·99
	21,894 ($^{n+1}P_y$)	86·11 (F_t)

Table (b) *Mortality and Survival Factors for the Study Area.*

	One year Mortality rates		*Quinquennial Survival factors*	
Age	*Male*	*Female*	*Male*	*Female*
0	0·03056	0·02328	—	—
1–4	·00114	·00094	0·9943	0·9953
5–9	·00062	·00031	·9969	·9984
10–14	·00052	·00031	·9974	·9984
15–19	·00072	·00042	·9964	·9979
20–24	·00104	·00052	·9948	·9974
25–29	·00125	·00073	·9937	·9963
30–34	·00177	·00114	·9912	·9943
35–39	·00260	·00177	·9870	·9911
40–44	·00437	·00291	·9782	·9854
45–49	·00728	·00457	·9637	·9771
50–54	·01206	·00707	·9401	·9646
55–59	·02037	·01091	·8992	·9454
60–64	·02547	·01819	·8743	·9090
65–69	·04886	·02911	·7615	·8544
70–74	·07640	·04802	·6321	·7599
75–79	·11279	·07900	$(0{\cdot}8872)^5$	$(0{\cdot}9210)^5$
80–84	·16840	·12214	$(0{\cdot}8316)^5$	$(0{\cdot}8779)^5$
85 and over	·23129	·18971	$(0{\cdot}7687)^5$	$(0{\cdot}8103)^5$

Table (c)

Quinquennial migration totals by age group for 300 persons per annum net flow

	Persons	
Age	*Male*	*Female*
0	29	28
1–4	40	38
5–9	51	51
10–14	51	51
15–19	54	51
20–24	111	93
25–29	120	108
30–34	126	99
35–39	75	66
40–44	66	42
45–49	42	27
50–54	24	21
55–59	9	12
60–64	3	6
65–69	3	3
	804	696

5

Projection of the Study Area's Employment

At regional level, one of the factors underpinning the population of the region is the volume and nature of employment opportunities offered by its industrial structure. The same is true in a more dynamic sense. Where a steady growth of population has been forecast for the region, there must be at least an implicit assumption that there will be a comparable growth in employment in or adjacent to the region. Conversely, where a tight local labour market exists, any expansion of employment will only be possible if there is a supporting increase in local population of working age. The existence of commuter flows to and from outside the region blurs, but in no way weakens the inter-relationship between population and employment at local level.

The previous chapter provided projected figures for population to the target years of 1976 and 1981; the purpose of this chapter is to complete the estimates of purely internal growth by projecting the employment offered by the local economy to those years.[1] Obviously, some estimates of employment are necessary, both to provide a check on the viability of the population forecasts – if only to direct local objectives towards the provision of supporting employment where necessary – and also to allow planners to formulate their policy on spatial zoning for industrial, residential and other uses.

Forecasting changes in employment, even at national level is a hazardous business, involving as it does such diverse variables as internal and international pressures on demand and output, changes in technology and their rate of acceptance over the period, and the effects of population growth and age structure on both demand and supply sides. The difficulties are compounded when forecasts have to be made for a small sub-region such as the Study Area, where the changes in its employment pattern will be influenced by both national and local factors. No area will reflect completely, industry by industry, the pattern of national changes over the period; equally, no area will be totally unaffected by significant changes in the nature and level of the economic activity of the nation. Nevertheless, while the problems

[1] The previous chapter discussed the problem of conflicting growth forces and concluded that, for the Stirling Study Area, there was no indication that external development would constrain internal expansion. If the opposite had been true, projections of internal expansion would have to be adjusted for this.

involved in employment projection cannot be ignored, so long as the exercise provides even broad guidance on possible future changes in the local economy it is an important part of the assessment of impact on the region.

The Method of Projection

The essential feature of any conventional method of projection of employment is that it will be based on observation of past and present industrial structure characteristics of the region. At its simplest, the projection approach attempts to judge the extent to which these characteristics will continue to hold true in the future. This approach is most clearly illustrated in the projection method which, assuming that the local economy is quite independent from the national economy, establishes the past trends of growth and decline in local industries over some past period of normal change, and extrapolates these trends, either as compound rates of annual change or as absolute numbers, into the future.[2] For very short term forecasts, where local industrial structures are unlikely to vary significantly, this simple approach can be quite adequate. However, care must be taken to avoid excessively mechanical extrapolation of trends by industry, i.e. these trends should be adjusted in the light of any current knowledge of local patterns of change for the future.[3]

The main weakness in any purely local approach to projection has been referred to earlier, in that it is unlikely that any local economy can remain isolated from the national climate of economic activity. The past trends in local employment which provide the basis for the extrapolation are likely to have been affected, at least to some extent, by national upswing or downturn; again, the state of the national cycle is likely to impinge on the local forecast for the future.

Recognition of this inter-relationship between national and local changes in employment, coupled with the existence of more extensive data on forecasting at full national level, has influenced other writers[4] to use projection models based explicitly on national/local relationships. The method of approach here, is to examine past trends of local growth and decline by industry in employment terms, and compare these to the national performance of the same industries over the period in question. This allows an

[2] See J. T. Hughes, 'Employment Projection and Urban Development', *Regional and Urban Studies*, ed. S. C. Orr and J. B. Cullingworth.

[3] For an illustration of this method of projection, see J. T. Hughes study of Edinburgh and the Lothians in chapter 10, *The Lothians Regional Survey and Plan*. For a discussion of other mainly local base methods, see his chapter on 'Employment Projection and Urban Development'.

[4] For example, see K. J. Allen and S. C. Orr in chapter 4, *The Grangemouth/Falkirk Regional Survey and Plan*, Vol. 1.

analysis to be made of the way in which local industries perform consistently better or worse than their national counterparts. Next, use is made of a national employment projection; this is applied to the local industrial structure and corrected for local divergence from the national pattern, as observed in the past. Once again, as with the simpler method, care must be taken not to project too mechanically; allowance must be made for any anticipated local factors which might alter the national/local relationship identified from the past. Equally, flexibility in the use of national forecasts is essential, and where these appear to be seriously in error for a particular industry, from actual statistics which post-date the forecast, some modification of the estimated rates of change may be necessary.

Employment Projections for the Stirling Study Area

While several approaches are available which allow the combination of national and local influences in the forecast, a fairly simple approach was adopted for the Stirling Study Area. This method, developed from a technique used in Chapter 3, projects the employment pattern of the Study Area on the basis of estimated national changes in industrial structure for the period 1961–76, as modified for normal local residuals and adjustments to particular industries. In estimating the national change in industrial structure over the period, a choice existed between using the National Plan[5] or the broadly similar estimates made by Beckerman and Associates in *The British Economy in 1975*. Despite the official abandoning of its target, the Plan can still be used as a reasonable guide for future rates of relative growth between industries. Both the Plan and the Beckerman estimates have used, broadly, the same approach for the projection, basing this on estimates of final demand and total output by industry, with allowances for productivity improvements and changes in the composition of the labour force. The Beckerman estimates were chosen, partly because they were more detailed and partly because they covered virtually the same period as the first stage in the employment projections for this chapter.[6]

The explanation for the differences normally experienced between national and local rates of change over a period tends to be found, to a great extent, in the relative composition of the industrial orders. An increase of 12% in national employment in Engineering and Electrical Goods, where the employment bias is towards the 'light' engineering and electronics, is unlikely to be reflected in an area where engineering employment is mainly engaged in the manufacture of agricultural machinery. Given these differences in the

[5] The National Plan, September 1965, Cmnd 2764, as updated by *The Task Ahead*, H.M.S.O. for D.E.A., 1969.

[6] See Table 5.1, page 50, column (*b*) for the Beckerman estimates of change.

structure of industry within the S.I.C. Orders, it can be assumed reasonably that a local area will perform consistently better or worse (in terms of growth or decline in employment) than the nation as a whole, over the short and medium term,[7] i.e. there will tend to be a steady plus or minus residual from the national trends of employment change. Estimates were made[8] of these residuals from employment data for the U.K. and the Study Area for the period 1960–68, and a correction, or modification factor[9] calculated for each industry, to adjust the estimated change in employment from national factors to the actual figures recorded for the end of the period.

As the first step in projecting employment for the Study Area to 1976, the Beckerman estimated changes for the period were applied to the employment structure of the Study Area at the beginning of the period to provide the national component of estimated employment for 1976. Next, assuming that the modification factors for 1961–76 would be the same as for 1960–68 these estimates were corrected for local influences to provide a preliminary series of estimates of employment by industry for the Study Area for 1976.

At this stage, there were two main sources of error in the projections; firstly, the projected national rate of change could be in error and, secondly, changes could have taken place in the relationship between national and local trends, i.e. in the modification factors. For example, in Mining and Quarrying, there has almost certainly been a change in the value of the modification factor, which, over the 1960–68 period, reflected the series of closures of collieries and N.C.B. workshops. These closures were the last major redundancies in mining locally, and from 1971/72 there will be considerable employment in the newer collieries opened to serve the Longannet Power Station. For this industry in the period to 1976, neither the national trend nor the modification factor will apply; for both 1976 and 1981, it is estimated that employment will remain constant at about 3,250 men from the Study Area. Again, in the case of Food, Drink and Tobacco, the national trend estimate of a 4% decrease in employment over the period compares to an actual 3% increase in employment nationally to 1968; accordingly the Beckerman figure has been adjusted to a 4% increase over the period. Also in this industry, the modification factor for 1960–68 reflects an inter S.I.C. Order transfer and has been adjusted to allow for this.[10] Taking account of both adjustments, the preliminary figure for employment in this industry has been amended to 2,090 persons for 1976.

[7] The sluggish response of changes in regional industrial structures to post-war attempts at diversification indicates how difficult it is to change significantly industrial composition over the short and medium term.

[8] See Appendix A for statistical sources and the method of estimation of both the residuals and the modification factors.

[9] Modification factors show the extent to which the actual change in the Study Area will exceed (M.F. greater than one), or fall short of (M.F. less than one) the national rate of change.

[10] See Chapter 3, section on Trends of Growth and Decline.

Further adjustments to either national trend or local modification factors have been made to Engineering and Electrical Goods, Bricks, Potteries and Glass, Construction, Insurance, Banking and Finance, Professional and Scientific Services, and Public Administration and Defence. When the final projected figures for persons employed by industry in the Study Area for 1976 are totalled, the total labour force of 39,655 represents an increase over the period of 6%. This compares to the Beckerman estimated increase in the national labour force over the period 1960–68 of 6·7% and the implicit increase in the National Plan, extended for an equivalent period, of over 7%. On past trends, the relationship between local and national increase seems to be just about right; in the past, the Study Area labour force has grown slightly faster than the Scottish one, which, in turn, has performed rather worse than the U.K. labour force, in terms of employment growth.

One difficulty in methodology remains. In estimating the pattern of employment in the Study Area in 1976, some of the original Beckerman estimates of employment have been increased, in view of the apparent divergence of estimated and actual changes in national employment, or, when applied to the Study Area adjusted for further changes in modification factors. While these adjustments seem defensible when taken individually, overall they might give rise to inconsistencies. If more people are employed in a given sector than was originally estimated, then less must be employed elsewhere than estimated to maintain overall balance in the changes estimated for the labour force. In fact, comparison of the actual and Beckerman estimated changes in employment for the mid-point in the period of the projection, indicates that there has been a fair degree of compensation between industry groups. While some industries have experienced a considerably greater increase than estimated, in others, e.g. mining, shipbuilding, the rate of contraction has been rather greater than anticipated; equally, other industries have expanded less than forecast, or have even declined. Thus, if adjustments were made for actual changes by the mid-point of the period, they would tend to compensate, and at least a rough balance would be maintained.

The projected employment figures for 1976[11] indicate that Mining and Textiles, the two largest industries at the beginning of the period, will decline markedly over the period, both in terms of relative importance and numbers employed. This decline will be more than offset by increases in employment in most of the other industries, particularly, Professional and Scientific Services, Construction and Distributive Trades. The projections indicate a further shift towards the Services sector, relative to Primary and Manufacturing sectors.

Projections for employment in the twelve main industries have been made to 1981, with the remaining industries projected as a single group. The

[11] See Table 5.2, page 51, for comparison of projections in the main industries for 1976 and 1981.

method of projection used, bearing in mind the problem of falling accuracy over a longer period which faces any method, has been to assume that the relative direction and magnitude of employment changes for 1961–76 will continue to be experienced to 1981; figures for that year have been extrapolated by straight line trend from the 1961–76 employment figures. As a result of this they merely show a continuation of the trends in overall structure, as observed for 1976, with a further increase in the relative importance of the Services sector.

The various employment figures for 1976 or 1981 show that, even ignoring the impact of the University and its secondary growth on the local pattern of employment, marked changes in the industrial structure of the Study Area are likely to take place with a continuing decline in the relative position of the traditionally important industries, a continuation of the trends experienced for 1951–66. For the future, as for that earlier period, the most rapidly expanding sectors will be Services industries, a conclusion supported both by national expectations and by the type of population increases projected earlier in the chapter. The extent to which the development of the University will accelerate these trends is examined later.

Table 5.1 *Projection of Employment Structure to 1976*

S.I.C.	*Base population average 1960–62* (*a*)	*Beckerman estimates 1960–75* (*b*)	*National estimates for Study Area* (*c*)	*Modification factor* (*d*)	*Estimated employment 1976* (*e*)	*Adjusted* (*f*)
1. Agriculture	681	−29·76%	478	1·014	485	485
2. Mining	5,044	−43·32	2,859	0·893	2,553	3,250
3. Food, Drink and Tobacco	2,398	−3·53	2,313	0·839	1,941	2,090
4. Chemical	17	+25·89	21	0·824	17	17
5. Metal Manufacturing	52	−4·04	50	0·745	37	37
6. Engineering	1,503	+11·98	1,683	0·941	1,584	1,686
7. Shipbuilding	15	−3·60	14	0·667	9	9
8. Vehicles	89	+4·10	93	0·146	14	14
9. Metal NES	1,070	+2·33	1,095	0·972	1,064	1,064
10. Textiles	4,346	−10·60	3,885	1·017	3,951	3,951
11. Leather	32	−0·59	32	0·167	5	5
12. Clothing	27	−0·59	27	1·375	37	37
13. Bricks etc.	1,340	−4·08	1,285	1·229	1,579	1,759
14. Timber	420	+0·95	424	0·642	272	272
15. Paper	1,569	+10·44	1,733	0·979	1,697	1,697
16. Other Manufacturing	413	+13·73	470	0·774	364	364
17. Construction	2,899	−2·05	2,840	1·094	3,107	3,663
18. Gas, Electricity etc.	880	+41·64	1,246	1·116	1,391	1,391
19. Transport	1,719	−2·07	1,683	1·002	1,686	1,686
20. Distribution	3,612	+22·41	4,421	0·962	4,253	4,253
21. Insurance	502	+10·27	554	1·266	701	815
22. Professional etc.	2,995	+10·27	3,303	1·095	3,617	4,896
23. Miscellaneous Services	3,138	+10·27	3,460	0·999	3,457	3,457
24. Public Administration	2,652	+20·87	3,205	0·829	2,657	2,757
Total	37,413	+6·72			36,478	39,655

Table 5.2

Estimates of Employment Structure in the Study Area

S.I.C. Order	*1961*	%	*1976*	%	*1981*	%
II. Mining	5,044	13·5	3,250	8·2	3,250	7·9
X. Textiles	4,346	11·6	3,950	10·0	3,850	9·4
XX. Distribution	3,612	9·7	4,250	10·7	4,450	10·9
XXIII. Miscellaneous and other	3,138	8·4	3,450	8·7	3,600	8·8
XXII. Professional etc.	2,995	8·0	4,900	12·4	5,500	13·4
XVII. Construction	2,899	7·7	3,650	9·2	3,950	9·6
XXIV. Public Administration	2,652	7·1	2,750	6·9	2,800	6·8
III. Food, Drink etc.	2,398	6·4	2,100	5·3	2,000	4·9
XIX. Transport	1,719	4·6	1,700	4·3	1,650	4·0
XV. Paper, Printing	1,569	4·2	1,700	4·3	1,750	4·3
VI. Engineering etc.	1,503	4·0	1,700	4·3	1,750	4·3
XIII. Bricks, Glass etc.	1,340	3·6	1,750	4·4	1,900	4·6
All other industries	4,198	11·2	4,500	11·3	4,600	11·2
	37,413		39,650		41,050	

APPENDIX A

Estimation of Local Modification Factors for 1961–76

The method chosen to project the employment pattern of the Study Area was to apply a series of national estimated rates of change to the employment structure of the local area at the beginning of the period and then correct these preliminary estimates for local influences. The figures chosen for the national estimates are discussed in the chapter. This appendix is concerned with the estimation of the local residual component, as based on the comparison of national and local changes in employment over the period 1961–68. A straightforward comparison of the figures for these years could result in residuals of false magnitude, partly reflecting regional differences in the impact of cyclical trends and partly as the result of, say, a coincidence of an industrial dispute with the June count figures for persons in employment; where one of the areas to be compared is rather small, like the Study Area, local disturbances can distort employment figures significantly. To avoid this, the figures for employment by S.I.C. Order for the beginning of the period were taken as the average of the persons employed in each industry for 1960–62, and the end of the period figures as the average of 1966–68.

The first step in the calculation was to find the national rate of change by industry for the period.[1] This was then applied to the Study Area employment structure for the beginning of the period[2] to estimate persons employed by

[1] See column (*c*) to table 1 for this appendix.
[2] See column (*d*) – the average figures for 1960–62.

the end of the period solely on national trends.[3] These figures were then compared to the actual[4] numbers of persons employed, and the difference expressed as a modification or correction factor from the national change figures.[5] The value for the modification factor was calculated by dividing the actual numbers by estimated numbers employed in the industry. The modification factor for Bricks, Potteries and Glass, of 1.229 shows that, for the period 1960–68, the actual numbers employed were 22·9% greater than forecast by national trends. Alternatively the modification factor of 0·839 for Food, Drink and Tobacco were 16·1% less than estimated by the national trend, i.e. 83·9% of the national figure.

[3] See column (*f*).
[4] The actual figures are given in column (*e*).
[5] See column (*g*).

Table 1 *Estimation of Local Modification Factor*

	U.K. ('000 Persons)			S.A. Persons			
	Average ('000) 1960–62	*Average ('000) 1966–68*	*Percent charge*	*Average 1960–62*	*Average 1966–68*	*National Δ applied to 1960–62*	*Modification factor*
	(*a*)	(*b*)	(*c*)	(*d*)	(*e*)	(*f*)	(*g*)
1. Agriculture	619	460	−25·69	681	513	506	1·014
2. Mining	746	552	−26·01	5,044	3,332	3,732	0·893
3. Food	842	864	+2·61	2,398	2,065	2,461	0·839
4. Chemicals	532	522	−1·88	17	14	17	0·824
5. Metal	622	608	−2·25	52	38	51	0·745
6. Engineering	2,139	2,373	+10·94	1,503	1,568	1,667	0·941
7. Shipbuilding	277	215	−22·38	15	8	12	0·667
8. Vehicles	905	838	−7·40	89	12	82	0·146
9. Metal NES	559	589	+5·37	1,070	1,096	1,127	0·927
10. Textiles	895	779	−12·96	4,346	3,849	3,783	1·017
11. Leather	64	59	−7·81	32	5	30	0·167
12. Clothing	597	538	−9·88	27	33	24	1·375
13. Bricks etc.	351	363	+3·42	1,340	1,703	1,386	1·229
14. Timber	295	322	+9·15	420	294	458	0·642
15. Paper	620	650	+4·84	1,569	1,610	1,645	0·979
16. Other Manufactures	309	352	+13·92	413	364	470	0·774
17. Construction	1,558	1,689	+8·41	2,899	3,437	3,143	1·094
18. Gas	389	432	+11·05	880	1,090	977	1·116
19. Transport	1,685	1,661	−1·42	1,719	1,699	1,695	1·002
20. Distribution	2,912	2,940	+0·96	3,612	3,510	3,647	0·962
21. Insurance	569	669	+17·57	502	747	590	1·266
22. Professional	2,110	2,680	+27·01	2,995	4,163	3,803	1·095
23. Miscellaneous Services	2,071	2,220	+7·19	3,138	3,359	3,364	0·999
24. Public Administration	1,318	1,438	+9·10	2,652	2,398	2,893	0·829
	22,984	23,813	+3·61	37,413	36,907	37,563	0·983

6

The Regional Income Multiplier Model

The analysis of the economic effects of introducing a new source of employment into a region poses a number of intriguing problems in regional economics. Some of these are concerned with the extent to which the new project will affect its local economy; its influence may be marginal, or again, in terms of direct employment offered and indirect employment generated, quite considerable, depending upon such factors as the local industrial structure, the size of the project and the extent to which the latter stimulates local trade flows. On a more theoretical level, there is also the problem of choosing the specific method of analysis to be used; the economic repercussions involved can be analysed by a number of methods, each with its advantages and disadvantages.[1]

A first possible approach towards measuring the impact of a new industry on the region would be to estimate and apply an export base multiplier to the new direct employment. The export base multiplier has been extensively used in urban planning, particularly in America,[2] and operates on the identification of two main sectors of industry and employment in the local economy. One sector, the 'export base', or 'basic' sector, produces goods and services for consumption primarily outside the region; its level of output, i.e. the region's exports, is set by demand forces from outside the region and will grow or decline depending upon the behaviour of that external demand. The other sector, the 'servicing' or 'non-basic' sector, produces goods and services which are consumed within the region; this sector supports, or services, the basic sector and the persons employed in it. The export base approach hypothesises that a fairly stable relationship exists between the two sectors, with any expansion or contraction of the 'basic' sector being reflected directly onto the 'servicing' sector. If 'basic' employment constitutes a steady proportion of total employment, a ratio, or multiplier value, can be calculated empirically to show how many 'servicing' jobs are supported by each 'basic' job. This multiplier value can then be applied to any new employment received in the basic sector, to estimate secondary or indirect employment generated by this.

[1] A detailed explanation will be given only for the income multiplier approach. The export base and input – output approaches have been surveyed extensively elsewhere and are dealt with only in broad outline in this chapter.

[2] See *Methods of Regional Analysis*, W. Isard, chapter 6, for a fuller discussion of the export base approach and a bibliography of American studies which have used this method.

The criticisms of this appealingly simple method are well known. In reality, it is often extremely difficult to identify the industries of the 'export base', since some 'export' industries have part of their output consumed locally and some 'non-base' industries possibly export part of their output. The picture is further complicated by the desirability of including some backward linkage industries, such as component suppliers and other key service industries, in the export base. Again, the approach, in its simpler forms, assumes too passive a role from the servicing sector where, in practice, employment can change of its own accord as a result of, say, investment from private industry or the public sector. Further, as with most multipliers, there is the problem of stability of the ratio between the sectors over time, in the face of changing productivity within and between industries. Finally, of these broad criticisms, the income multiplier model deals more clearly with such factors as the various feedback effects discussed later, the problem of transfer earnings in a local economy, and the interplay between income and employment generation.

A second possibility and at first sight, the most detailed framework against which the impact of a new project could be measured, would be an Input-Output analysis of the local economy. Ideally, this approach would allow a formal study to be made of the production and distribution characteristics of the individual industries (or, more realistically, the main industries) of the region, as well as their trading inter-relationships between each other and, particularly where the region is small, with other regions; against the detail of an input-output table, the effects and repercussions of the establishment of a new industry, such as the University, could be traced.[3] However, the construction of such a table, even for a highly simplified matrix of the main industries, would involve an immense expenditure of effort and time, due to the problem of data availability, collection and processing. Even when constructed, the model would be open to criticism on the set of industries chosen, the data used, and the accuracy and stability of the coefficients which have been calculated.[4] Not even the use of national coefficients, adjusted for local characteristics by selective data collection,[5] seems to offer a satisfactory solution to the cost and time problems involved.

At least one writer[6] has been moved to comment that regional input-output models have all the problems of national models, plus some additional ones of their own. The use of the input-output technique for the Stirling

[3] This type of approach was used by Blake and McDowall (*Scottish Journal of Political Economy*, November 1967) to study the contribution of the University of St Andrews to the local economy; more recently, the University of Aberdeen are using input-output techniques to study the impact of the aluminium smelter at Invergordon.

[4] See Isard, *Methods of Regional Analysis*, chapter 8, section C.

[5] See S. Czamanski and E. E. Malizia, 'Applicability and Limitations in the use of national input-output tables for Regional Studies', *Regional Science Association Papers*, Vol. 23, 1969.

[6] Meyer, *Regional Economics, Surveys of Economic Theory II*, p. 255.

study was rejected, partly for the same problems discussed above, but mainly because it was felt that the main objective was not to analyse in depth the economic structure of the region, but to asses only the economic affect of a new regional project. This study of change at the margin can be dealt with by the regional income multiplier, which has rather less detailed and voluminous data requirements and needs a less rigorous knowledge of inter-industry and inter-regional relationships.[7]

The impact of the University on the population of the Stirling Study Area will depend on its impact on employment, both direct[8] and secondary; while direct employment will be governed by teaching and other considerations, the amount of indirect employment generated will depend upon the income received and spent within the Study Area by those directly employed.[9] Effectively, the critical area of impact is the income injected into the local economy by the University, together with its subsequent expenditure. It is in the analysis of this aspect of the growth of the University that the regional income multiplier model can be used; once the impact on income has been quantified, the final estimates for employment and population can follow.

This chapter is concerned with the development of a multiplier model to analyse the income effect of the University. Firstly, it discusses the basic theory of the income multiplier; next, it surveys the series of papers which have appeared recently in British journals on multiplier models, and comments on the results obtained; thirdly, it attempts to bring together the main suggestions made and develop these ideas and relationships into a completed model; fourthly, it selects the multiplier values to be used for the model and provides further estimates of some of the main terms in the model; and, finally, it provides a more generalised form of regional multiplier model for use in impact studies elsewhere.

The Basic Multiplier Formulation

The basic theory of the income multiplier is simple enough; a money injection into an economic system, whether national or regional, will cause an increase in the level of income in that system by some multiple of the original injection,[10] i.e. where ΔY_r represents the change in the level of the

[7] In fact, while it is normally, as in Isard and Meyer, presented as an alternative method of analysis to input-output, the regional multiplier approach can be used as a simplified input-output system, by developing the conventional multiplicand.

[8] Direct employment excludes construction workers on the University site.

[9] And on the Local Value Added component of the University's construction expenditure – see later.

[10] For non-economists, the multiplier approach adds together the income generated by the various rounds of expenditure within a community. The size of the multiplier is governed by the severity of the leakages of income from that community, since it is only the income flow remaining in the local economy which can generate further income. In more illustrative

region's income, J the injection and k_r the value of the regional multiplier, then,

$$\Delta Y_r = k_r J$$

The conventional formulation of the multiplier (k_r) assumes that the level of Investment (I), Government ecpenditure (G) and regional exports (X) will remain constant and autonomous, then makes allowance for the various leakages during the multiplier process, such as the proportion of the additional income consumed (c), direct taxation and National Insurance contributions (t_d) decline in transfer payments with the rising level of regional income (u), imported consumer goods (m) and indirect taxation (t_i); conventionally, the problem of undistributed profits is ignored in the simple model. These symbols for the various marginal propensities, with the usual relationships, provide the basic formulation towards which all the papers move, despite differences in the approach taken:

$$k_r = \frac{1}{1 - c(1 - t_d - u)(1 - m - t_i)} \tag{2}$$

Survey of Current Literature

In recent years there has been a considerable wave of interest in formulating and estimating values for regional income multipliers, to allow some evaluation to be made both of the usefulness of this analytical method and, through it, of the consequences of regional stimulation policies. The main contributions on the model have been made by Professor Archibald,[11] Professor

---

terms, the money injection into the local economy might take the form of a new car purchased by an immigrant to the area, e.g. a member of academic staff in the Stirling case study. A large part of this first round of expenditure will spill directly from the local economy as the garage pays for the car which will have been imported to the area, and for the indirect taxation on the car. Only the residual becomes the income of the garage and is distributed to owners and employees. Here again it is subject to further leakages before it can be spent, in the form of direct taxation dedicted from income, and household savings from net of tax income. It is only the income flow surviving all these leakages which passes back into the local economy in the form of a second round of expenditure. Once again, this will be greatly reduced by the cycle of leakages of income from the area, with only the residual passing through to the third round of expenditure, and so on until the expenditure rounds become insignificant. If the initial *source* of income generation was £1,000 spent on the car, the income residuals of the various rounds of expenditure might add up to, say £400. The multiplier, which is the *process* of income generation, has added a further £400 to local incomes. In terms of equation (1), the total increase in regional income (ΔY) is £1,400, made up of the initial injection (J) of £1,000, multiplied (k.) 1·4 times.

[11] 'Regional Multiplier Effects in the U.K.', G. C. Archibald, *Oxford Economic Papers*, March 1967.

Brown and colleagues,[12] Professor Wilson,[13] K. Allen,[14] D. B. Steele[15] and M. A. Gr eig.[16]In all cases, these papers set up basic models and, in most use these to provide estimates of the multiplier effects of various types of projects; having done so, most then suggest ways in which the model might be improved. These suggested modifications fall into two categories, those affecting the basic multiplier formulation and those affecting the formulation of the multiplicand.

Generally speaking, the basic multiplier model set up in most of the papers is either similar to or covers the same types of leakage as the model shown in equation (2). The only basic model to differ substantially[17] from this is the one developed by Greig. This model is particularly interesting, inasmuch as it deals with the impact of a new project on a sub-region, whereas the other models relate to standard planning regions. Secondly, it caters for an inflow of a large body of immigrants to the area to work in the new industry and analyses their effect on indirect employment generation in both private and public sectors. This regional case study is obviously very similar to the study of the impact of the University.

This immigrant inflow situation has given rise to two main modifications to the conventional model. Firstly, the multiplier process has been separated into a first round of expenditure (of income received from the project), and the other rounds of the multiplier. Since the income received from the project accrues to immigrants to the region, the important factor becomes the overall expenditure pattern of these; for this first round, average rather than marginal propensities are used, with the normal marginal propensities reverted to for all other rounds of the multiplier. The second modification is that an interaction between employment and income multipliers has been identified and is included in the model; the population growth associated with direct and the generated indirect employment increases the demand for public services and, therefore, generates further employment here, the income from which adds to the multiplier effects from the initial injection. Thus, the first round income multiplier (k_a) will have three components, namely income from the wages of direct employees, plus the proportion of this accruing to Local Value Added through expenditure, plus the income of the additional public employees, i.e.

[12] 'The "Green Paper" on Development Areas', Brown, Lind and Bowers, *National Institute Economic Review*, May 1967.

[13] 'The Regional Multiplier, a Critique', T. Wilson, *Oxford Economic Papers*, November 1968.

[14] *Regional and Urban Studies*, Ed. Orr and Cullingworth, pp. 80–96.

[15] 'Regional Multipliers in Great Britain', D. B. Steele, *O.E.P.*, July 1969.

[16] 'The Regional Income and Employment Effects of a Paper Mill', M. A. Greig, *Scottish Journal of Political Economy*, February 1971.

[17] The apparent differences of the Steele model have been caused largely by his amalgamated figure for savings and taxation leakages and the single coefficient value applied to this.

$$k_a = 1 + v + \frac{\left(E_d + \dfrac{\Delta V}{l}\right)\theta w_p}{E_d w_d} \tag{3}$$

where v is the proportion of the increase in income which is L.V.A., E_d represents direct employment, ΔV the increase in L.V.A. created by direct employees, l the increase in L.V.A. needed to create an additional job in the service trades, θ the ratio of public service to other employees, and w_d and w_p the average earnings of direct employees and public service employees respectively. For subsequent rounds, the marginal propensities to consume (c^*) and tax directly (t^*) are used. The autonomous item for Government expenditure (G) is split into an exogenous component (G') and an endogenous component (G^*), where the latter represents income paid to public service employees and where $G^* = \lambda Y$ (with λ being the income of public sector employees as a percentage of total income). Thus the multiplier for second and subsequent rounds (k_r) becomes:

$$k_b = \frac{1}{1 - \lambda - c^*(1 - t^* - u)(1 - m)} \tag{4}$$

and the overall regional multiplier (k_r) can be calculated as:

$$k_r = 1 + k_b(k_a - 1) \tag{5}$$

The remaining category of modifications are all concerned with adjustments to the formulation of the multiplicand and can be summarised as:

(a) a modification to include repercussions from inter-regional trade;
(b) a modification to take account of leakages from the injection; and
(c) a modification to include a feedback effect from induced investment.

The effect of modifying the multiplicand to incorporate repercussions from inter-regional trade has been analysed by Brown and Steele. The multiplied rise in the level of income in region A causes a rise in its level of imports (M_a) through consumption expenditure (C_a); this increase in imports to A becomes, for its non-international component, a rise in the level of exports from other regions in the country (collectively region B), i.e. an injection which raises, through the multiplier, their level of income (Y_b), consumption (C_b) and imports (M_b) in turn.[18] Some of this increase in imports will leak back to region A as an increase in exports, i.e. a further injection causing a further rise in income in A. If $M_b = m_b C_b$ and $C_b = cY_b(1 - t_d - u)$, than A's exports will rise by $m_b c Y_b(1 - t_d - u)$, and the effect of any injection on region A's income being:

$$\Delta Y_a = \frac{G_a + m_b c Y_b(1 - t_d - u)}{1 - c(1 - t_d - u)(1 - m_a - t_i)} \tag{6}$$

[18] From the Brown model, where Y_b etc. represent changes in the level of income etc. and not the absolute levels.

The increase in the level of income in region $B\,(Y_b)$ is generated by the change in the level of A's imports from B in the first place. With similar relationships as before, then, after the multiplier process:

$$Y_b = \frac{m_a c Y_a(1 - t_d - u)}{1 - c(1 - t_d - u)\,(1 - m_a - t_i)} \tag{7}$$

so that this can be substituted for Y_b in equation (6)[19] and the final multiplier for A becomes:

$$k_a = \frac{G_a\{1 - c(1 - t_d - u)\,(1 - m_b - t_i)\}}{\{1 - c(1 - t_d - u)\,(1 - m_a - t_i)\}\{1 - c(1 - t_d - u)\,(1 - m_b - t_i)\} - - \{m_a c(1 - t_d - u)\}\{m_b c(1 - t_d - u\}} \tag{8}$$

There is some disagreement as to whether this modification has any significant effect on the multiplier value; Brown argues that it only raises it slightly, from 1·28 to 1·29 for all Development Areas, whereas Steele estimates that it could raise the multiplier value by between 0·06 to 0·16, depending on the region. The clash of opinion seems to be due more to differences in the type of data used and the resultant coefficients, than the formulation of the model.

The second suggested modification to the conventional multiplicand follows from a point raised by Wilson, on the problem of injection leakages.[20] Conventional theory shows how the effect of an injection on a region's level of income will depend upon the nature and importance of the various leakages in the multiplier. Wilson pointed out that the injection itself was subject to leakages before undergoing multiplier expansion; if the industrial structure of the region was such that its capital goods industries were little developed, then it was conceivable that the only part of the injection to pass through to the multiplier would be the wages and salaries of construction workers. Thus, following Wilson, the modified multiplicand can be expressed as (my symbols),

$$\Delta Y_r = k_r J(1 - m^*) \tag{9}$$

where m^* is the direct leakage in imported capital goods. The importance of this modification is that, if the value of m^* is taken to be the same as m (in the multiplier), say 0·5, which is not excessively high, then

$$\Delta Y_r = k_r J(1 - m^*) < J \tag{10}$$

In other words, if there is a significant import leakage in the injection, then the final multiplied expansion of income could be less than the original expenditure on investment that gave rise to it.

[19] The Steele formulation, given the difficulties of comparison caused by his combined term S and its single coefficient value, appears to be similar to this.

[20] Wilson, op. cit., p. 378

The final modification to the conventional model, following suggestions made by both Archibald and Wilson, is to attempt to incorporate a feedback effect from induced investment. In the simple model, I and G are assumed to be constant and autonomous. Wilson[21] argued that, as income and expenditure rise through the multiplier, some additional investment is likely to be induced, particularly if excess capacity is not present. Taken with the type of formulation suggested by the Greig multiplier model, where the income generation process is based on the interaction of income, expenditure and additional employment generated in both private and public sectors, it is reasonable to expect induced investment on increased capacity in both sectors to support the employment thus generated. If induced investment does occur, its effect is to introduce a further component into the multiplicand, with obvious and, it has been argued, considerable effects on regional income levels.

The only attempt to include induced investment in the formulation of the multiplier model was made by Archibald.[22] Looking at induced investment in a situation where the initial injection or multiplicand took the form of wages and salaries paid to employees in a new project, all of whom were immigrants to the region, he argued that investment would be induced by the immigrants' expenditure; where (my symbols[23]) ΔN represents the annual induced investment in both private and public sectors and ΔZ the total annual earnings of immigrants, and where ΔN is functionally related to ΔZ,[24] then

$$\Delta N = n\Delta Z \tag{11}$$

Given the context of Archibald's analysis, his ΔZ is identical to the injection (J) used in the conventional multiplier model, so that he can elaborate on this simple multiplicand and include induced investment as

$$\Delta Y_r = k_r\Delta Z + k_r\Delta N \tag{12}$$

and, from equation (11), by substitution and rearrangement,

$$\Delta Y_r = k_r(1+n)\Delta Z \tag{13}$$

In assessing the results of the various models, taking first of all the various multiplier formulations, it would seem that despite the variety of approaches taken, both in algebra and in statistical data used, the final estimated values for k_r tend to group in a fairly narrow range. Archibald estimated in the preliminary stages of his paper that the value would lie somewhere between

[21] Op. cit., pp 379–81. [22] Op. cit., p. 37.

[23] Archibald uses the symbol ΔI for induced investment, although from his comments elsewhere in the article, he would seem to be including a ΔG element of induced public sector capital expenditure in it. I have changed the symbol to indicate that both sectors are involved.

[24] Archibald uses the immigration situation to avoid the functional relationship of $\Delta N = n\Delta Y$, where, given the formulation for the multiplier itself, the denominator may become negative (op. cit., p. 37, see footnote).

1·2 and 1·7, depending on a variety of factors; later he made a 'best guess' estimate that the value would be 1·25 for a typical standard region. Brown estimated a value of 1·28 for the Development Areas as a whole and about 1·24 for a very small region. Allen estimated that the k_r value for Scotland would be between 1·4 and 1·5. The Steele estimates of k_r for the various regions lie, excluding the Scottish figure, between 1·19 and 1·41; the Scottish figure, as a result of a remarkably low import leakage coefficient, was estimated at about 1·70 to 1·89. Greig's estimate, for the sub-region around Corpach gave the range as between 1·44 to 1·54; the relatively higher values for this small region follow from his modifications to the basic model. Overall, there would seem to be fairly general agreement that the value of the regional multiplier is likely to lie within the range 1·24 to 1·54. The actual value for any given region will depend on a number of factors, such as size, industrial structure and social characteristics, as these affect the various multiplier leakages, particularly the important import leakage.

Taking next the suggested modifications to the multiplicand, the effect of reformulating this to include feedback from inter-regional trade is, as mentioned earlier, somewhat under dispute but, at most, would only increase the range of estimates by 0·16. The other two suggested modifications would seem to be rather more significant. Allowance for import leakages in the multiplicand, as in equation (9) could reduce drastically the final multiplied expansion of income; on the other hand, the inclusion of an induced investment effect could increase considerably the final income expansion.[25]

Development of the Model

Given the broad agreement on the value for k_r it would seem that the most profitable area of future development would lie in the formulation of the multiplicand. In view of the relatively small economic base of the typical Study Area, it is argued that it is unlikely to cause or receive significant repercussions from inter-regional trade; the feedback effects from this source, as in equation (8), are therefore ignored in building up a model to analyse the impact of the University. On the other hand, given the duration of the construction activity on the University campus, the Wilson leakage modification should be incorporated. Equally, given the past levels of economic activity in the Stirling Study Area and taking even the most pessimistic of the population increases which have been projected, it seems unlikely that there is or will be any significant underutilisation of capacity in the area. Thus, following arguments advanced by both Wilson and Archibald, the gradual and prolonged rise in the level of income and expenditure associated with the

[25] Archibald argues, from equation (13) that if $n=1$ (my symbols), then the income change is double that estimated by k_r alone.

growth of the University, coupled with the considerable inflow of immigrants anticipated,[26] should induce a significant amount of additional investment in the area; the effects of induced investment must also be incorporated into the model.

The model which can be constructed from the suggestions made in the current literature would involve bringing together the suggested Wilson modification, as in equation (9) and the suggested Archibald modification for induced investment, as in equation (12), but this time in the context of a more normal situation where, as for the University employment, there is some proportion of non-immigrants on the staff of the new project (i.e. $\Delta Z < J$). Then:

$$\Delta Y_r = k_r J(1 - m^*) + k_r \Delta N$$

and, by substituting from equation (11),

$$\Delta Y_r = k_r \{J(1 - m^*) + n\Delta Z\} \qquad (14$$

Before attempting to estimate the values of these new coefficients m^* and n, it is clear that the modifications suggested need further analysis and re-definition.

Current literature has treated the multiplicand component for the initial injection, as opposed to the component for induced investment, as representing in some situations the investment expenditure on the construction and equipment of a new project in the region, in other situations as representing the income received in wages and salaries of staff employed in the continuing operation of the project and, indeed, in some cases as loosely representing both sources of regional income. Only Archibald appears to consider the effects of different types of injection, and even he does not examine the consequences of the combination of different types of injection. For most new regional projects, e.g. the Pulp and Paper Mill at Corpach, the new University of Stirling and the aluminium smelter at Invergordon, the J component of the multiplicand will have two elements. The first, J_1, will represent the construction expenditure involved in setting up and equipping the project. The second, J_2, will represent the continuing flow of income arising from the employment given by the project. In some circumstances, J_1 will cover only a year or so of expenditure and, since it will have, in theory, no permanent effect on the level of income,[27] can be ignored (as it was by Greig for Corpach, for which his model was effectively $\Delta Y_r = k_r J_2$). In other circumstances, e.g. the continuing period of 14 years of constructional activity associated with the development of the University of Stirling, to exclude it would be to understate the multiplied income effects of the project. Secondly, it is obvious that when considering the problem of injection

[26] Given the nature of the employment offered by the University.

[27] A typical example of this would be the postwar Hydro-Electric construction programme in the Highlands.

leakages, the Wilson modification should be applied to J_1 and not J_2, i.e. equation (9) can be rewritten as,[28]

$$\Delta Y_r = k_r J_1(1 - m^*) + k_r J_2$$

or,

$$\Delta Y_r = k_r\{J_1(1 - m^*) + J_2\} \qquad (9')$$

The importance of applying this import leakage to the construction expenditure component of J is that, since induced investment, as normally defined, relates to the construction of additional capacity in the Services sector (e.g. offices, shops, housing in the private sector and housing, schools, hospitals, roads etc. in the public sector), then a similar injection leakage must be applied to the induced investment component. Thus, depending on the value given to import leakages, the effect of induced investment on regional income generation could be considerably less than suggested. To restate the model, as given in equation (14), for these corrections

$$\Delta Y_r = k_r J_1(1 - m^*) + k_r J_2 + k_r \Delta N(1 - m^*)$$

which, by substitution and rearrangement becomes[29]

$$\Delta Y_r = k_r\{J_2 + (J_1 + n\Delta Z)(1 - m^*)\} \qquad (14')$$

Estimation of the Values of the New Terms

Equation (14′) provides the basic model which will be used to estimate the income and employment effects of the University on the Stirling Study Area. While developed for this purpose, it is nevertheless a model which is open to more general application and is capable of being used to assess the economic impact of any new project on the income level of the sub-region in question, e.g. the aluminium smelter at Invergordon. The values for J_1, J_2 and ΔZ will obviously depend upon the nature of each individual project, although a further examination of ΔZ will be made later in the chapter in view of the importance of this component of the multiplicand for regional income generation.

However, the effect of these components on regional income cannot be assessed without some idea of the possible values for n and m^*. Without doubt, the more difficult estimate is for the coefficient of induced investment (n), given the various problems to be taken into account in the estimation of regional capital-output ratios.[30] The actual induced investment for any new regional project will depend on factors such as the degree, if any, of excess

[28] By redefining this component, it would seem that it is less likely that $k_r J(1-m^*) < J$, given reasonable proportions for J_1 and J_2.

[29] In most cases, where J will be of a temporary nature, unlike the Stirling University case, then

$$\Delta Y_r = k_r\{J_2 + n\Delta Z(1-m^*)\}.$$

[30] Wilson, op. cit., pp. 385–87.

capacity in the Services sector mainly, the various lags involved in consumers' expenditure and suppliers' reaction, and the size and industrial structure of the region in question. To compound these problems, there is, predictably, the absence of almost the full range of necessary regional statistics, even at standard region level.

In the face of these difficulties, a much more simple approach was taken in the attempt to estimate a plausible value for n.[31] If $\Delta N = n\Delta Z$, then $n = \frac{\Delta N}{\Delta Z}$. Briefly, on the basic assumption that a figure can be taken for capital requirements per immigrant, and further assumptions made as to the period of time over which these capital requirements will be provided, then an annual value for ΔN can be estimated for the group of immigrants. Secondly, the annual value of ΔZ can be estimated by calculating the numbers of the group who will be economically active, and the average earnings per person of these. The value estimated for n was 2·4. Compared to the estimated national capital-output ratio of about 2,[32] this may seem a little high at first sight. However, it is argued that, while the estimate is undeniably tentative, in a regional situation of a considerable immigration inflow and a reasonable degree of utilisation of existing capacity, a ratio of this magnitude is not totally implausible. If this argument is accepted, it can be seen that both Archibald's and Wilson's comments on the effect of induced investment on a region's income were justified – given that these comments did not take account of import leakages from this component of the multiplicand; indeed, the former commented that '(the) multiplier effects of the migrant's wage are probably much less important than the multiplied induced investment his presence leads to'.[33]

The second necessary estimate[34] is for the value of the import leakage coefficient (m^*)from construction expenditure in the multiplicand and, in the light of the above comment, the importance of this leakage is obvious. Briefly, apart from the problem of obtaining adequate data, the main problem is that the magnitude of the leakage varies between the different cost elements in construction; Local Value Added can be virtually non-existent in some cost categories, e.g. overheads and capital equipment, but quite considerable in others, e.g. direct labour costs. Using data which reflected national as much as local experience, it has been estimated that the value for m^* will lie[35] in the range 0·7 to 0·8, although again this must be regarded as a tentative first estimate. Despite this, it would seem probable that import leakages from construction expenditure components in the multiplicand are

[31] See Appendix A.

[32] 'Long-term growth and short-term policy', W. A. H. Godley and J. R. Shepherd, *National Institute Economic Review*, August, 1964.

[33] Op. cit., p. 37.

[34] See Appendix B., page 73.

[35] It must be emphasised that this value relates to a sub-region rather than a standard region, where leakages would tend to be less.

relatively more serious than the import leakages experienced during the multiplier process, where m, for a similar size of region might lie between 0·6 and a maximum of about 0·7. A plausible explanation of this might be found in the unique characteristics of the construction industry, which tend to undermine what are conventionally regarded as the minimal L.V.A. components of mark-up on materials used and wages paid to construction workers. On the one hand, this industry tends to import the bulk of its materials from central depots to the region; on the other hand it also imports central teams of key workers as the core element in the labour force at any given site. By reducing its reliance on local purchases of materials and labour, the industry causes a relatively greater leakage than might be the case for other industries.

An import leakage of this magnitude has obvious and serious effects on the income generation potential of induced investment. Since this was brought into the model by the symbol ΔZ, i.e. annual immigrants earnings, some benefit can be gained from a further examination of this multiplicand component. Basically, three main points can be made. Firstly, only in extreme cases, e.g. where the labour reserves of the region have been entirely exhausted and the manning of new projects depends completely on immigrant labour, will the Archibald situation, where $\Delta Z \equiv J_2$ apply. Normally, ΔZ will be a proportion of J_2, varying with the dependence on immigrant labour, which might be minimal in some projects, when only key management and production training posts are filled from immigration, and very close to the Archibald situation in others. In all situations,

$$\Delta Z = zJ_2 \qquad (15)$$

Substituting this into the formulation of the model would give

$$\Delta Y_r = k_r\{J_1(1 - m^*) + J_2(1 + nz\{1 - m^*\})\} \qquad (14'')$$

which has the benefit of specifying more clearly the immigration source which induces the investment in question.[36] The second main point concerns the estimation of z for the individual project. It must be remembered that, given the assumptions on the time pattern of induced investment made in Appendix A, the annual total of induced investment is not related to the final proportion of J_2 earned by immigrants at the end of the period of immigration, but to the total earnings of any one year's group of immigrants to the project. Thus, if immigrants will ultimately make up 50% of the labour force after a five-year period of build-up, z is not $0{\cdot}5J_2$; if immigration is a steady inflow over the period, then z is $0{\cdot}1J_2$. To relate induced investment to the total annual earnings of all immigrants would be to overstate seriously the effect on regional income. To complete the second main point, since

[36] In the situation where J_1 is of a temporary nature and is ignored, then of course

$$\Delta Y_r = k_r\{J_2(1 + nz\{1 - m^*\})\}.$$

immigration to any project will typically be biased towards the more senior posts, z cannot be taken as the proportion of immigrant persons in the labour force, but must be weighted to take account of the higher income received where this is the case. For the purposes of the University model, the value of z will be estimated, along with J_1 and J_2 in the following chapter.

The third and probably most important point on induced investment is that since in the Archibald type of formulation it has been defined as constructional expenditure related to immigration, then, once the period of immigration to the project has finished and the capital requirements of the immigrants have been met, ΔN will drop out from the multiplicand,[37] as would J_1 at, presumably, an earlier stage, and the model will revert to the simple

$$\Delta Yr = k_r J_2 \tag{16}$$

For example, in analysing the impact of the University on regional incomes, there will be a steady build-up of staff and students from 1966 to the early 1980's, with immigration being a significant and steady inflow over the entire period and with there being no evident under-utilisation of capacity from the start. Here, the income multiplier effects of the University for any year during the period of growth would include feedback from induced investment; however, an estimate of income generation for, say, 1985, would be made not from the type of formulation of equation (14″) but from (16) above, since immigration will have ceased by this later year and, presumably, the capital requirements of even the final year's immigrants finally met.

It would seem that, at least in the context of the Archibald type of formulation, the effect of including induced investment in the multiplicand was not as great as was expected, even in the short and medium term. Nevertheless, during the period of immigration, the definition of the multiplicand, as given in equation (14″), i.e. to include values for both construction expenditure and induced investment, despite import leakages and the reduced 'z' value for induced investment, can still result in a significantly larger multiplicand than the more conventional model. For example, in the Stirling case study, taking m^* as 0·75, n as 2·4 and z as 0·1, the effect of including construction expenditure and induced investment in the multiplicand is to increase the value of this by about 20% of the more conventional multiplicand, J_2 – with all the resultant repercussions on income and employment generated.

In conclusion, the model developed for use in estimating the effect of the new University on regional income and, from this, employment and population, is as given in equation (14″), i.e.

$$\Delta Y_r = k_r\{J_1(1 - m^*) + J_2(1 + nz\{1 - m^*\})\}$$

[37] Or, at best, reduce to the annual depreciation on the additional capital stock.

The values for J_1, J_2 and z will be estimated in Chapter 7. The value of m^* has been estimated at 0·75 and n as 2·4. Two values will be taken for k_r to provide a lower case and an upper case estimate of the income impact. The lower case value of k_r will be taken from the Brown model and estimates for a small region, at 1·24; the upper case value will be taken from the Greig sub-regional model, with its immigrant modifications, at 1·54.

The Generalisation of the Multiplier Model

The model developed for the Stirling case study can be generalised quite simply into a form which is capable of being applied to projects elsewhere. The basic formulation used for the model then becomes:

$$\Delta Y_r = k_r(J_1 + J_2 + J_3) \tag{17}$$

Each of the multiplicand components, i.e. the various sources of income generation, must be stated net of leakages from the region. In this general form, J_1 represents the net annual expenditure on construction of the project, J_2 the ongoing income from staff salaries and wages and student revenue sources, and J_3 the net annual expenditure for induced investment.

It may well be that, for some projects, there is no justification for including values for J_1 and/or J_3; this will depend upon the circumstances surrounding the particular project and must be a matter of judgement. If this is the case, then the model reverts to the simple form of equation (16). Equally, the project's circumstances might suggest that other major sources of income generation exist and should be included in the multiplicand. Even in the Stirling model, it would have been possible to add annual values for rent received for vacation letting of residences (J_4), annual expenditure on maintenance contracts (J_5) or annual expenditure on internal security (J_6). To include these, the model could have been broadened to

$$\Delta Y_r = k_r(J_1 + J_2 + J_3 + J_4 + J_5 + J_6) \tag{18}$$

In fact, these additional terms were ignored, partly because heavy leakages left them relatively insignificant (particularly J_5 and J_6) and partly because double counting adjustments virtually cancelled them out (the staff employed in the residences have their income included already in the J_2 component, and cannot also be included in J_4).

However, the basic principle remains, in that the more general form of the model can be stated as

$$\Delta Y_r = k_r(J_1 + J_2 + J_3 + J_4 + \ldots + J_n) \tag{19}$$

to include, for any given project, all significant sources of income generation, so long as these are stated net of all leakages from the region, and double counting (i.e. incomes etc. included elsewhere) is avoided.[38] It is quite possible that some new industries might have strong linkages with other indigenous industries, and that their introduction to the local economy might cause a substantial increase in employment in these local industries. In these cases, it is essential to include in the multiplicand the related injections of net income which can be attributed clearly to the major industry.

Finally, having dealt with the sources of income generation, the process of income generation is covered by the value of the income multiplier (k_r). While a specific value can be set for any given region, provided that all the coefficients of the multiplier can be estimated for that region, in most cases, it should be sufficiently accurate to use a range of probable multiplier values. For most normal areas, with some immigration to the new project, such a range could be set from a lower multiplier value of, say 1·30 to an upper multiplier value of, say 1·45. This broad central range, which could be modified if any exceptional circumstances exist[39], will tend to provide a realistic range of income generation estimates, from which employment and population estimates can later be derived.

APPENDIX A

Estimation of the Value of the Induced Investment Coefficient

This estimate can only be made on two basic assumptions, firstly that existing Service capacity in the region is already fairly fully utilised and, secondly that immigrants to the region will have the same relative capital requirements as the population for the U.K. as a whole. Ideally, estimates of capital requirements should be based on data gathered from each region. However since the full range of statistics needed for even as simplistic an approach as this, is available at only U.K. level, rather than mix national with particular local statistics, the former have been used throughout although obviously items such as activity rates, earnings and specific type and quantity of capital required will vary between any region and the nation as a whole. In defence, it is argued that the purpose of the estimate is not to provide a definitive value for induced investment but only a plausible value which will give some idea of the importance of this additional component of ΔN in the multiplicand.

Capital required per immigrant is calculated in Table (a) to this Appendix. The estimates of total U.K. population and of net capital stock at current

[38] For an illustration of the use of this type of multiplicand see M. A. Greig's report to the Highlands and Islands Development Board of the economic impact of investment in fisheries.

[39] If the area depends heavily on goods imported from outside its boundaries the multiplier range of values should be lower. If it is strongly self-sufficient, with fewer goods than normal imported, the range should be raised.

replacement cost[1] are given for 1964–68, permitting the estimation of the net capital stock per person in the U.K. – a far from perfect, but nevertheless usable proxy for capital requirements per immigrant. The figures given for this are comparable to the Mishan/Needleman[2] estimate of capital requirements per immigrant household.

While the provision of these capital requirements in the receiving region involves induced investment in both private and public sectors (i.e. $\Delta I + \Delta G$) unlike Mishan and Needleman, no attempt will be made to allocate ΔN between these sectors, on the grounds that any allocative device would be arbitrary and that such a distinction is quite unnecessary for analysing the effect on total income of induced investment feedback.

Having estimated the total figure for capital requirements/induced investment per immigrant the next stage is to estimate the annual total for capital provision for a group, of say 1,000 immigrants to allow its inclusion in the multiplicand. It is unlikely that the capital requirements of an immigrant will be met in full within his first year of residence in an area. Mishan and Needleman assume that the provision will take place over a two-year period; Archibald, having considered this period, appears to opt for a three-year period. If this larger period is taken and it is further assumed that the capital is provided in an even flow over the period, then for any given immigrant, or group of immigrants, 1/3 of their capital will be provided in any year. If, however, it is further assumed that there is an even flow of immigrants for each year of the period over which the immigration takes place, then after a three-year build-up, the total for capital provided levels off at a figure equal to the total capital requirements for any single year's group of immigrants. Thus ΔN, as an annual figure for any year after the first three of the period of immigration, is not 1/3 of the estimate in Table (a) but is the full amount. If one takes a group of, say, 1,000 immigrants to any region, then using U.K. rather than local statistics for that group, the estimated annual figure for ΔN are given in the first column of Table (b).

The second main stage in the calculation is to estimate the total annual earnings for that group of immigrants over the same period. To estimate ΔZ, a calculation must be made of the number of that group likely to be in paid employment and a further calculation made of how much, on average, each will earn in a given year. Keeping to U.K. statistics, it would be possible to estimate the number employed by applying U.K. activity rates to the immigrants. This would be unsatisfactory; research work on migration flows indicates that the typical age structure of migrants is rather younger than that of the nation as a whole. The application of normal U.K. activity rates

[1] Net of accrued capital consumption, sources given at foot of table; see also *National Account Statistics, Sources and Methods*, pp. 383–4.

[2] L.B.R., July 1966 – although their capital requirements figure was used for a different purpose.

would therefore under-state total earnings. To avoid this, it was assumed that the migrants have the same age and sex characteristics as indicated by the 1966 Sample Census returns; the resultant breakdown is given in Table (c). To this breakdown were applied age and sex specific activity rates for the U.K.[3] to give a total activity rate for the immigrant group for each year of the period, as shown in Table (d), and from the numbers employed.

The figure for average earnings has been taken from the Blue Book statistics of Personal Incomes before Tax,[4] rather than the Survey of Personal Incomes in the *Abstract of Regional Statistics* in view of some of the technical difficulties involved in use of the latter. The average income can be estimated from dividing the total number of incomes into the figure for total personal income before tax, for each year. If it is assumed that the employed immigrant in any year received this U.K. average income figure, then average earnings per immigrant for 1964/67 (latest figures available) can be estimated as in column 3 of the Table (d). Column 2 multiplied by column 3 gives the total estimated ΔZ for the group of 1,000 immigrants for each year of the period.

Having estimated for this group ΔN and ΔZ over the period, the final step is to compute the estimated value of the coefficient for induced investment over the period (where $n = \Delta N/\Delta Z$). These estimates are given in column 3 of Table (b) and range from 2·40 to 2·48, with a mean value of 2·43.

Thus it has been estimated that $n = 2{\cdot}4$. Since this is based on average U.K. statistics which will not relate to any single region with its own figures for existing capacity, its own industrial structure, its own particular needs for additional capital provision, its own age and sex structure of migrants, its own level of earnings, it is obvious that this value can only be taken as a tentative first estimate of a plausible value for a regional capital and output ration in the circumstances of immigration to a new major project in the region.

A final point relates to methodology. Given the method used to estimate ΔN the capital requirements of immigrants to the University, it might be argued that this involves an element of double-counting, in that the construction of the University represents the provision of part of these capital requirements. Firstly, since ΔN was estimated by dividing the net capital stock of the U.K. by the estimated population of the U.K. to obtain a net capital stock *per capita* figure, the construction of the University adds to capital stock and is therefore part of ΔN. Secondly, induced investment represents an increasing of capacity in private and public sectors; the University provides not only educational services, but also campus shops, restaurants and social clubs and, in doing so, must substitute to some extent for increased capacity in induced investment.

It is argued that, in the first case, whereas a school would service a small

[3] *Abstract of Regional Statistics* 1968, table 9; 1969, table 11.
[4] 1968, table 26; 1969 table 23.

local area and would qualify entirely for capital provision under ΔN, a University services not so much a local community as the nation as a whole (only 5% of students are expected to be local by the end of Phase 2). Thus, the construction expenditure on the University cannot be allocated entirely to the local community, but must be shared nationally – when the annual *per capita* figure becomes £0·27; such an adjustment to a *per capita* figure of about £1,500 per annum would be insignificant. The second argument advanced is far more important; the extent to which staff and students use the service facilities provided by the University will reduce the pressure on capacity elsewhere and therefore the need for induced investment in sectors outside the University. Rather than adjust the value for ΔN, or n, since the University situation is unique and would not normally be experienced in the impact from a project, the method of adjustment chosen has been to establish the share of J_1 which represent the average annual expenditure by the University on the provision of these services and deduct it from J_1. The multiplier effects of the construction of this capacity on campus will then be applied to the induced investment component, i.e. is included in the values estimated for this. By stating J_1 net of this deduction, double-counting has been avoided; the adjustment is made in Chapter 7.

Table (a) *Estimates of Capital Needs of Immigrants*

	Estimation of population in U.K. (1) (millions)	*Net capital stock at current replacement cost* (2) £millions	*Net capital stock etc. per capital* £
1964	54·01	69,700	1290·5
1965	54·36	76,700	1411·0
1966	54·65	82,400	1507·8
1967	54·98	87,400	1589·7
1968	55·28	93,300	1687·8

Sources:

1. *Annual Abstract of Statistics*, 1969, table 6.
2. *National Income and Expenditure*, 1969, table 62.

Table (b) *Estimation of Value of Coefficient for Induced Investment*

	Estimate of annual capital requirement provision (ΔN)	*Estimate of annual earnings* (ΔZ)	*Estimate of induced coefficient* $\left(n=\dfrac{\Delta N}{\Delta Z}\right)$
	£millions	£'000	
1964	1·291	536·4	2·41
1965	1·411	583·3	2·42
1966	1·508	627·3	2·40
1967	1·590	641·1	2·48
1968	1·688	NA	NA

Table (c) *Age and Sex Structure of Immigrant Group of 1,000*

	Male	*Female*
Under 15	114	112
15–24	110	96
25–44	258	210
45–64	52	44
65 and over	2	2
	536	464

Table (d) *Estimates of* ΔZ

	Activity rates for immigrant group %	*Immigrants employed*	*Average earnings per person* £	*Total earnings of immigrant group of 1,000* (ΔZ)
1964	53·3	533	1,006·3	£536,358
1965	53·5	535	1,090·3	583,311
1966	54·2	542	1,157·4	627,311
1967	53·1	531	1,207·4	641,129
1968	—	—	NA	NA

APPENDIX B

Estimation of the Value of Import Leakages (m^*) from the Multiplicand

Two components of the multiplicand will be affected by import leakages, firstly and more obviously, J_1 expenditure, i.e. the original construction expenditure on the new project, and secondly the construction expenditure involved in the induced investment component (ΔN). While there is some reason to expect that the import coefficients might vary betweem the two components (e.g. J_1 may involve the construction of highly specialist industrial premises, with ΔN involving mainly additional capacity in retail distribution etc., schools, hospitals, housing, roads), as a first approximation, it is assumed that a 'general' import leakage coefficient can be applied to both components.

Obviously, the type and volume of this type of constructional imports will vary between regions, reflecting in particular the type of industrial structure in the region and the geographical location of the region in relation to constructional supplies. Ideally the value for m^* applicable to any region should be based on local data for that region's construction industry on the various cost elements of direct material, direct labour, plant etc. Once again, however, for the area around the University of Stirling at least, difficulty in collecting or even obtaining access to local data has resulted in basing the estimates as much on 'average' national data as on local figures and experience. While this is unsatisfactory, it does provide an offset in that the value of m^* estimated will be capable of more general application since it will not be completely distorted by any uniquely local characteristics. The statistics used are a combination of national cost structure figures for the industry and local data of both formal and confidential, and informal nature. Again, the remarkably wide spread of constructional activity in the region, covering construction of University premises, housing (private and public sector), shops and office premises, schools, roads etc. does help to provide a fairly plausible general value for m^*. Since no attempt, as yet, seems to have been made to estimate any empirical value for m^*, even this type of general approach is not without interest.

The method used was to break down construction expenditure/receipts into the various cost components and attempt to estimate the L.V.A. content of each of these, gathering the latter together into a final estimate of $(1 - m^*)$. The average cost breakdown used by the industry and based on national experience is:

	%
Direct materials	30
Direct labour	30
Plant etc.	30
Overhead and profit	10
	100

The practice apparently is that these 'rule of thumb' proportions are then adjusted in the light of the type of construction work to be completed, e.g. industrial premises or housing, if the latter whether high-rise or low-level etc. In view of the wide range of activity around the University, it was felt by civil engineers and others involved in the industry, that the overall breakdown would be fairly close to these average proportions (in fact, for this particular area and type of work, they suggested that materials would account for slightly more (about 35% at most) and capital equipment slightly less (about 25% at least) than the average breakdown). If the average figures are taken then it will tend to reduce the effect of unique local activity on the import estimate.

Taking materials first, L.V.A. here will cover materials used which were purchased or manufactured locally. If the area around the University is taken as a typical sub-region then the only local manufactures would seem to be the high-volume low-volume purchases of shale and quarry materials for grounding work. It would seem from local construction firms that this accounts for well under 5% of total material costs; say about 3%. As regards local purchases, it is obvious that there is a marked difference in policy between main contractors and sub-contractors; the former have central depots and import virtually all materials into the sub-region from these, whereas the latter, being typically more local-resident in nature, seem to rely much more on local purchases. For the construction work in general in the district there appears to be a 60:40 breakdown between main and sub-contractors. Taking main contractors first (and excluding expenditure on local sand, gravel etc. which has already been counted) it would seem that about 10% of the total direct material costs are from local purchases; but since these local purchases are of goods held locally but already imported to the sub-region, only the margin, say 20% is L.V.A., i.e. only 2% of the direct material costs of the main contractors is L.V.A. Further, using the 60:40 breakdown as a weighting device, this will then account for only 1·2% of the total direct material costs for the industry. Sub-contractors, on the other hand, appear to purchase about 2/3 of their materials within the sub-region: applying the same margin to this, only about 13% of their direct material costs are L.V.A. weighted for the 60:40 breakdown, this becomes 5·4% for the direct material costs at industry level. Thus, taking manufactures and purchases together, the L.V.A. component accounts for only about 10% of direct materials costs, i.e. about 3% of total construction expenditure.

Much the same problem of differing behaviour between main and sub-contractors apply to direct labour costs. Main contractors have a central core of permanent workers in a district and move teams from this central pool into the various sites; these 'core' teams are then augumented by local labour while they themselves commute daily to the site from often quite considerable distances (a round trip of 50/60 miles daily is not uncommon to the area around the University). While practice varies between firms, a fair average would seem to be that main contractors recruit about 60% of their men locally (including the local element in the 'core' teams); this will account for about 36% of total direct labour costs for the industry. Sub-contractors employ about 75% of their labour force from local sources, bearing in mind that some of these smaller firms are highly specialist and may be hired from considerable distances outside the area; given 60:40 breakdown this will account for about 30% of total direct labour costs. Thus, in total about 66% of direct labour costs are L.V.A. or about 20% of total construction expenditure.

Plant and equipment costs are relatively simple to deal with from the point of view of estimating L.V.A. content. From local evidence, all plant and equipment used in site preparation or construction generally is either hired from firms outside the area or brought in the sub-region from outside depots by both main and sub-contractors. Thus this cost element has a zero L.V.A. content.

The most unsatisfactory data obviously concerns the L.V.A. content of overhead and profit. For main contractors, there is a total leakage of both from the area. For sub-contractors, it has been impossible to gather any information directly and the only guidance has been received second-hand from civil engineers and main contractors. On the basis of it, it would appear that, at best, about 50% (possibly as low as 40%) of overhead and profit receipts remain in the area as L.V.A. If the guestimate of 50% L.V.A. is taken, then for the entire industry, this amounts to 20% of the total of this cost element, or 2% of total construction expenditure.

Thus to summarise, the L.V.A. content $(1 - m^*)$ for the various types of construction costs would seem to be

	%
Direct materials	3
Direct labour	20
Plant etc.	0
Overhead and profit	2
	25

From this it can be seen that m^* can be estimated at 0·75. Obviously the more developed is the construction industry in the sub-region's industrial structure, the lower will be the value for m^*; conversely the more J_1 expenditure relates to specialist capital equipment or ΔN to specialist civil engineering the less likely it will be that any sub-region – or even standard region – can supply this from within and the greater will be the value of m^*. A 'normal' range, allowing on the one hand less leakages in overhead and profit, some local plant, materials etc. to the more severe position of specialist work, might give m^* a range of about 0·7 to 0·8, i.e. still significantly above the relative size of import leakages from the multiplier itself.

7

The Impact of the New Project on Local Income and Employment

The previous chapter discussed the formulation of the basic income multiplier model. This chapter, firstly, illustrates how the various multiplicand components are computed for the target years, and how the impact of the new industry on local income levels is measured. Secondly, illustrates how these estimates and the data gathered in making them can be extended into further estimates of direct and indirect employment provided and generated by the new industry. Finally, it suggests a method by which the two types of employment can be allocated as a growth component within the local industrial structure.

The basic approach used to estimate the income and employment effects of the University, is capable of being applied to any new development. The general form of the models used can be adapted to take account of any unique characteristics of the project and/or the receiving region. However, the actual process of computation used in the Stirling case study, being related to a specific situation, will of necessity be rather more detailed and difficult to relate directly to other studies. Even so, the case study detail which follows should provide general assistance to other studies, if only in illustrating how the problems of leakages and double-counting associated with any project can be identified and have allowance made for them. The great danger of the multiplier approach is that, in outline and in its basic formulation, it has a deceptive simplicity. It must be recognised that the accuracy of its estimates and the further estimates of employment made from these, depends utterly on the careful computation of the multiplicand components (the *sources* of income generation) and their separation from the multiplier's expenditure rounds (the *process* of income generation). Great care must be taken to identify clearly the various types of income leakage and the stage at which they occur.[1] Equally, where some inter-relationship exists between the multiplicand components, this must be analysed carefully,

[1] As a general rule, if these leakages (apart from P.A.Y.E. deductions which are adjusted in the multiplier itself), occur before the income is spent for the first time in the local economy, it should be adjusted in the multiplicand; if they occur at any time subsequent to this, they will normally be covered by the K_r formulation.

to avoid counting twice into the multiplicand a given source of income generation.[2] Any major errors in this computational stage will not only affect the accuracy of the estimated effect of the project on income; where employment and population estimates are derived in part from the income figures, these errors will be carried through the entire analysis.

The Effect of the University on Local Income

In Chapter 6, it was argued that the formulation of the multiplier model would depend upon the stage of growth of the University. While the University was continuing to grow, with a steady stream of immigrants coming to it for employment, the model will include, in addition to ongoing wages, salaries etc., terms for both construction expenditure on the campus and the investment induced in the local economy by the expenditure pressures of University employees and students; this formulation is given in equation (14″). On the other hand, when the University has completed its growth, both campus construction work and construction work on local induced investment will cease. Both these terms, in such a situation, must be dropped from the multiplicand, and the multiplier formulation reverts to the simpler form of equation (16).

It is suggested that it is helpful to select target years for the estimates which cover both types of situation, i.e. mid-growth and end-growth. Estimates made on this basis will provide a fuller picture of the effects over time of the new project.

The target dates chosen for the Stirling case study have been based on the various growth phases planned for the University.[3] In outline, construction work on the University began in 1966 and the first intake of students was for the 1967–68 academic session. Growth since then has been and in the future will be limited by the constraints of the construction programme. As a result of this, Phase 1 of the planned growth in student numbers involved annual intakes until 1970–71 of about 200 first-year students; the economic effects of this period were obviously marginal and have not been analysed. Phase 2 growth commenced with the completion of the next stage of building in this year, and over this phase the annual intake of students will rise to about 1,000; by 1976, the total student population of the University will be about 3,800, and employment will be given to an estimated 440 academic

[2] See, for example, the problems of residences staff, or the adjustment made for campus shopping facilities and their effect on induced investment, as discussed in Appendix A to Chapter 6.

[3] The original planning is contained in the University of Stirling Development Plan Report of 1968; these figures were amended by later policy decisions of the University and the more up-to-date figures are given here.

and 930 other staff. Phase 3 growth makes provision for the development of the University to an ultimate student population size of about 7,000, and the employment of about 2,700 staff of all grades. It was originally expected that the University would be asked to achieve this size by about 1981.[4] While, for a number of reasons, this no longer seems likely,[5] the date has been retained as a focal point for internal and University growth. The estimates of University impact for this year should, however, be taken to represent the ultimate effect which it will have on the local economy once its growth process has been completed[6] and it has achieved its final size.

Thus, the model to be used in estimating the impact of the University on local incomes at the recognised mid point in its growth, namely 1976, is given by equation (14″) in Chapter 6, where

$$\Delta Y_r = k_r[J_1(1 - m^*) + J_2(1 + nz(1 - m^*))]$$

when the value for the term 'z' is given by the equation[7]

$$z = \frac{\Delta Z}{J_2} \qquad (20)$$

Since values have already been estimated[8] for n and m^*, and lower and upper case values set for k_r, the remaining values to be computed in this section are for J_1 (the annual expenditure on construction work on the University campus for 1976), J_2 (the annual total income figure for 1976 of all income of staff and students), and ΔZ (the annual earnings of immigrants to the University in 1976).

The construction expenditure of the University in 1976 covers the construction of teaching buildings, residences and the campus in general, plus the expenditure involved in equipping and furnishing these premises, once they have been constructed. While a J_1 component is present over all stages

[4] See the Interim Development Plan, 1966, paragraph 2.12.

[5] The original figures were based on the Robbins Report on Higher Education, 1963, Cmnd 2154. Now, partly because of the growth in places from the established Universities and partly because of a decision that continuing rapid expansion could impose further considerable strains on the new University of Stirling, it seems likely that the ultimate size will be reached by a slower expansion path beyond the size of 4,000 students.

[6] In the present situation, it is extremely difficult to set any date by which growth will be completed. The only consequence of this for the final size estimates is that the number of University dependants will increase through births, net of deaths. The method by which this can be dealt with is discussed in Chapter 8. A more serious problem, raised by the uncertainty of the final size date, is concerned with the statement of the overall position of employment and population for the local area, as discussed in Chapter 9. If the date by which the final size is achieved is significantly later than 1981, say 1991, then the forecasts of internal population and employment growth given in Chapters 4 and 5 will have to be extended to cover this extra period. However, while this affects the detail of the Stirling case study, it does not affect the more general illustration of the methodology used. It is for this reason that the 1981 target year has been retained.

[7] This follows from the statement given in equation (15) of Chapter 6 that $\Delta Z = zJ_2$.

[8] See Chapter 6, Appendices A and B respectively.

of University growth, its annual value will fluctuate over the period. Discounting the more unrepresentative of the Phase 2 years,[9] it has been estimated that the average annual expenditure around the target year of 1976, taking both U.G.C. and Appeal Fund sources into account, will be about £1·31 millions, in 1969/70 constant prices.

The second component of J_1 represents expenditure on furnishing and equipment. While this obviously fluctuates with the completion phases of the various buildings, the University estimates that it will amount to between £250,000 and £350,000 per annum at constant 1969/70 prices by 1976. The actual figures taken is of little consequence. Firstly, only minimal purchases of furnishing items have been and will be made from local sources. Secondly, the technical equipment, by its very nature, has had to be imported in its entirety to the local area and provides no source of income generation for the local economy. In total, the import content accounts for 98% of total expenditure on these items, leaving only an annual figure of about £7,000 to be added to J_1.

The final adjustment to J_1 represents a double-counting problem. Part of the annual expenditure figure, estimated at about £66,000, is allocated to the provision of various service facilities used by staff and students, e.g. staff-student staff club facilities, restaurants, coffee lounges and shopping facilities on the campus. To the extent to which these are used by staff and students, this will involve a reduction in the expenditure pressure on local capacity, i.e. a reduction in the total of induced investment. In effect, it is a provision of part of this capacity within the campus.[10] To avoid double counting this source of income generation in the multiplicand, it has been deducted from J_1, reducing this to a final estimated figure of about £1·25 millions by 1976. It will be taken into the multiplicand in the induced investment figures.

The figure for J_2 has two separate components, namely the wages and salary bill of staff directly employed at the University (j_a) and the income of students from its various sources (j_b), both for 1976. The staff income estimate can be made from estimates of the staff numbers to be employed in the various staff grades by 1976, together with estimates of the average income for each staff grade.[11] The current estimates for this period suggest that about 1,400 staff will be employed by 1976. Taken with the estimates made[12] of the average incomes of the various staff grades (at constant 1969/70 prices[13]),

[9] Construction expenditure was particularly low for the first two years; it only assumed normal proportions when work commenced on the main new teaching complex.

[10] See Appendix A to Chapter 6 for a more detailed discussion of this point.

[11] See Table 7.1, page 87, for the detailed estimates of staff and income.

[12] This average income has been weighted by the expected seniority profile for each grade.

[13] The estimates throughout are in terms of constant 1969/70 prices to avoid the major problem of estimating the future rate of inflation and its effect on money wages and other cost elements.

these employees will inject a total income of £1·95 millions per annum into the local economy.

The estimation of a figure for total student income for 1976 is rather more complex a problem. Student numbers, on the basis of the revised current plans, can be taken as 3,432 undergraduates and 368 postgraduates. The main problems all lie in estimating the average student income figures. Firstly, allowance must be made for the three sources from which students might receive income, i.e. grant-paying authorities, parental contributions and vacation earnings. Secondly, allowance must be made for leakages from the local area in the form of students commuting to the University from outside the Study Area. Thirdly, for the majority of students who are resident on the campus, the average income must be stated net of rent paid to the University. There are two reasons underlying this latter adjustment: firstly, a proportion of student's rent is remitted directly from the local area by the University as capital and interest repayments on the loans incurred for the construction of the residences (as such it can create no further local income); secondly, the remainder of rent receipts is used by the University to pay the wages and salaries of the staff connected with the residences (and is therefore already counted in the j_a component). After these adjustments, it has been estimated that the annual total net income of the 3,800 students in 1976 will be, at constant 1969/70 prices, about £1·20 millions.[14]

However, there is one final deduction to be made for double-counting, before the J_2 figure can be computed. This represents the expenditure of staff and students on catering and other facilities offered on the campus. Part of the receipts from this is used by the University to pay the wages and salaries of the staff employed to provide these services (and, again, is already counted in j_a). The remainder either leaks from the local economy in the purchases of drink, foodstuffs etc., virtually none of which come from local trade flows, or is absorbed by the University to cover other operational costs. After adjustments for this final source of double counting and leakages, the final figures for j_a and j_b become £1·87 millions and £0·84 millions respectively, yielding an estimate of £2·71 millions for J_2 for 1976.

While, in some situations, the Archibald approach of assuming ΔZ to be identical to J_2 can be taken (e.g. the effect of a new project on the Midlands, with their low levels of unemployment and virtually exhausted labour reserves), in most cases, as with the University[15] a significant proportion of direct employees will be non-immigrant. For the University, experience has shown that the actual proportion of immigrants will vary between the types of staff; some (e.g. cleaning and catering) will be recruited virtually exclusively

[14] See Table 7.2 for a more detailed breakdown of this figure. A survey shows that most students spent most of their vacation earnings outside the region, bringing only a small balance back to the campus – hence the rather small contribution from this source.

[15] Particularly for Development Area projects, which are normally established to absorb local labour, even if key technical and management posts have to be filled with immigrants.

from local labour, whereas others (e.g. academic and senior administration and other staff) will be almost entirely immigrant.

Briefly, the estimates of total ΔZ for each grade of staff and students[16] were based on the current and anticipated future patterns of recruitment and admission. For non-academic staff, given the bias of immigration in the past to the more senior posts, the number of immigrants was weighted by salary scales to avoid understating earnings. Finally, the time pattern of the immigration was established and the estimates for the resultant annual flow of immigrants made; the annual total earnings for the year's inflow of immigrants was estimated at £243,000 (at constant 1969/70 prices) for 1976. Since $\Delta Z = zJ_2$,[17] for the purposes of the model, the value of z can be estimated at $0{\cdot}09J_2$.

Filling in the values of the various terms in the model,[18] it has been estimated that, in the lower case, the increase in regional income generated by the University will be £3·93 millions and the upper case increase £4·88 millions, both at constant 1969/70 prices. By 1976, the effect of the University will be to add between about £4 millions and £5 millions to the income level of the Stirling Study Area.

It is interesting to compare these estimates to those which would have been made by the other types of model which were discussed in Chapter 6. Dropping the component for induced investment and taking only $(J_1\{l - m^*\} + J_2)$ as the multiplicand, i.e. expanding the conventional multiplicand to include construction expenditure, as adjusted for import leakages, the estimated range becomes £3·75 millions to £4·65 millions; the exclusion of the component for induced investment, weakened as it is by the assumption of a time pattern for investment and the heavy import leakages involved, reduces the estimated income generated by about 5%. While it still provides a significant boost to the multiplicand, the importance of induced investment is not nearly of the magnitude suggested by many of the writers on multiplier theory. Finally, if construction expenditure is also dropped from the multiplicand and only the conventional J_2 retained, the estimated income range becomes £3·36 millions to £4·17 millions.

The series of estimates given above underlines the importance of specifying clearly the multiplicand relating to the project. The effect of including values for construction expenditure and induced investment, despite their heavy leakages, in the case of the University, is to increase the size of the conventional multiplicand by 17%. The inclusion of these terms increases substantially the estimated impact of the project on both income and employment generation.

Finally, the estimates of the effect of the University on local income levels, once it has completed its growth and achieved its final size of about 7,000

[16] See Table 7.3, page 88.
[17] Chapter 6, equation (15).
[18] See Table 7.4, page 88, for a summary of the values.

students, can be made from the simple model given in equation (16) in Chapter 6, namely that, for 1981

$$\Delta Y_r = k_r(J_2)$$

The terms for construction expenditure and induced investment have both been taken from the multiplicand for this year, on the argument that the construction work on the campus, and the immigration flows to the University, will both have been completed.

With J_2 for 1981 estimated as £5·19 millions at constant 1969/70 prices, and retaining the same lower case and upper case values as before for the multiplier (k_r), it can be estimated from the model that the completed University will add between £6·5 millions and £8·0 millions per annum to the flow of income in the local economy.

The Effect of the University on Local Employment

The estimation of the effect of a new project on local income levels should be of interest to more than merely the academic economist; the rise in income and the expenditure which will be associated with this will be of direct relevance to local traders and, indirectly via the reactions of these, to local planners. However, there can be little doubt that the main interest of physical planners and many others will lie in using the income figures as a point of departure for further estimates of the impact of the project in the more practical terms of employment and population. It was probably with this in mind that Professor Wilson argued the need to develop the income multiplier approach into an operational model for the guidance of physical planners.[19] This section of the chapter illustrates the first stage of this type of conversion by translating income into indirect employment generation terms.

The overall effect of the University, as a specific project, on employment levels in the local economy, will be made up of, firstly, direct employment in the various staff grades of the University, secondly, in the additional jobs offered in the construction work on the University campus and, thirdly, in the direct employment generated around the University in the local servicing sector.[20] Numbers for direct employment have been estimated in the previous section.[21] This leaves estimates to be made of the employment in construction and of indirect employment in the local economy for 1976.

Total construction expenditure for 1976 has already been estimated as

[19] T. Wilson, 'The Regional Multiplier: A Critique', *Oxford Economic Papers*, November 1968, p. 375.

[20] The term 'servicing' here is closer to the export-base definition than the normal S.I.C. Order Service Industry category.

[21] See Table 7.1, page 87.

about £1·25 millions. From data obtained elsewhere,[22] it can be assumed that 30% of this, about £375,000, will represent wages paid to construction workers. Since the average earnings of construction workers in Scotland for 1969/70 were about £1,220 per annum, this would seem to indicate a total labour force in University construction of about 310 workers in 1976.

The indirect employment generated by the University can be estimated in either of two ways. If fairly crude estimates of employment from this source are sufficient, the same simple approach can be used as was taken by Brown,[23] when he estimated the employment generation effects in Development Areas which might follow the introduction of the Regional Employment Premium. Firstly, the difference between the final income generated and the original multiplicand (as netted for its various leakages) must be calculated. This represents the additional income stemming from the various expenditure rounds of the multiplier process. Next, it is assumed that this additional income will have the same pattern of distribution as U.K. factor incomes, which allows an estimate to be made of the income figures which will be the 'Income from Employment' share. This share, representing the estimated income of indirect employees, is then divided by a cost per job, or average income figure (which should reflect the type of employment which will be generated by the project) to yield an estimated range of indirect employment of, for the Stirling case study, 850 to 1,690 jobs.[24]

A more satisfactory approach to estimating indirect employment is to use an employment multiplier.[25] The employment multiplier model chosen for the Stirling case study was developed by Greig[26] to analyse a similar type of project and its resultant immigration flow, with a similar type of receiving area. Apart from the advantage that it was constructed to deal with the same basic type of project impact, the Greig model has the further advantage in that almost all of its data requirements can be met from the information gathered to provide the earlier income estimates.

The Greig employment multiplier estimates total indirect employment (ΔE_i) in two stages; firstly it estimates indirect employment arising from the first round of expenditure (ΔE_a) then adds to this as estimate of indirect

[22] See Appendix B to Chapter 6, where the breakdown of construction expenditure into its different cost elements is given.

[23] A. J. Brown and colleagues, 'The Green Paper on Development Areas', *National Institute Economic Review*, May 1967, p. 30.

[24] The upper and lower limits of the range have been influenced partly by using the lower and upper case income estimates of the previous section, and partly by building into the average income figure a pessimistic weighting for employment generation in the lower case, i.e. a higher income figure per job, as against the current local average income figure used in the upper case.

[25] The employment multiplier is an export-base type of device which states the relationship between direct and total employment. An employment multiplier value of 1.5, say, implies that each 10 direct jobs generate a further 5 indirect ones.

[26] M. A. Greig, 'The Regional Income and Employment Effects of a pulp and paper mill', *Scottish Journal of Political Economy*, February 1971.

employment generated by the second and subsequent expenditure rounds (ΔE_b). ΔE_a is made up of the additional public service employees needed by the new direct employees, ($E_d\theta$) and, secondly, of additional employees in the private sector $\left(\frac{\Delta V}{l}\right)$ and, thirdly, the additional public service employees required by these, i.e. $\left(\frac{\Delta V}{l}.\theta\right)$ so that:

$$\Delta E_a = E_d\theta + \frac{\Delta V}{l}(1 + \theta) \qquad (21)$$

The indirect employment in second and subsequent rounds of expenditure, (ΔE_b), is estimated from taking the additional income from these stages of the multiplier, ($E_d w_d(k_a - 1)(k_b - 1)$), and dividing this by an income figure reflecting the additional income needed to create an additional job in the private (l) and public (w_p) sectors so that:

$$\Delta E_b = \frac{E_d w_d(k_a - 1)(k_b - 1)}{l(1 - \theta_1) + w_p\theta_1} \qquad (22)$$

his final model is that:

$$\Delta E_i = \Delta E_a + \Delta E_b$$

$$\Delta E_i = E_d\theta + \frac{\Delta V}{l}(1 + \theta) + \frac{E_d w_d(k_a - 1)(k_b - 1)}{l(1 - \theta_1) + w_b\theta_1} \qquad (23)$$

Using this employment multiplier formulation[27] it has been estimated that, by 1976, the University's growth will have generated indirect employment in the local servicing sector of, in the lower case 900 and, in the upper case, 1740 jobs. When the earlier figures for direct employment at the University, and construction work on the campus, are added to this, the final estimate for 1976 is that the University will add, in total, between 2,580 and 3,420 additional jobs to the local employment structure.

By 1981, construction work on the University will have been completed and there will be no further employment given by this component. The effect of the University on employment by then will consist only of direct employment at the University, and the indirect employment generated in the secondary growth around it in the local economy. It has been estimated that, when it achieves its final size, the University will offer direct employment to about 2,700 persons. Using the same employment multiplier approach as before, it can be estimated that the indirect employment total associated with the University will have grown to between 1,600 and 3,100 jobs. When it achieves its final size, therefore, the University should add between 4,300 and 5,800 jobs to the local employment structure.

[27] See Appendix A to this chapter for a more detailed explanation of the various terms in the Greig model and for the modifications which have been made to the basic formulation to provide lower case and upper case estimates for the University case study.

The Nature of the Additional Employment

While it is probable that, for most purposes, the broad estimates of magnitude for the additional employment, as given above, might be of sufficient interest to planners, it is possible to provide a further rough breakdown of these figures, to give some indication of the industrial nature of the new source of demand for labour. The employment generated directly and indirectly by the University can be broken down[28] into the same S.I.C. Orders which were used in the earlier chapters, on the basis of two assumptions. Firstly, it is assumed that the indirect employment created by the University will follow the same S.I.C. pattern as the probable pattern of the expenditure of the University incomes, since the employment will be generated by this expenditure. Secondly, it is assumed that the expenditure pattern of the total income of University staff, students and construction workers will be similar to the Scottish one, as given by the Family Expenditure Survey, averaged over the years 1967–70. Having allocated indirect employment in the same pattern as the expenditure pattern which emerged, the totals are grossed up by adding Construction employment to S.I.C. Order XVII and direct employment at the University[29] to S.I.C. Order XXII.

As a result, it was estimated that in the lower case, the University would account for just over half of the total employment figure of 2,580, with Distributive Trades (accounting for 18% or 477) and Construction (15% or 382 persons) as the next two largest industrial groups. In the upper case allocation, since the figure for University employment is unchanged, the University proportion falls to about 40% of the total; the next two largest groups remain Distributive Trades (27% or about 920 persons) and Construction (13% or about 450 persons).

As predicted, the main employment impact of the University will be felt by the Services sector, which will, by 1976, account for between 47% and 48% of the labour force of the Stirling Study Area, since about 83% of the employment from the University source has been estimated to fall in this sector. However, the analysis does indicate that about 17% of the additional employment will be in Construction and Manufacturing, mainly. Equally, employment in Services will not be exclusively in the Distributive Trades – a conclusion often explicit, or implicit, in the other forecasts of employment effect.

The breakdown of employment has not been extended to the 1981 figures; if desired, these could be computed in the same manner

[28] See Appendix B to this chapter for a fuller discussion of the method of allocating direct and indirect employment to S.I.C. Orders.

[29] The Department of Employment allocate by Workplace and not by Occupation; all University employment, under the 1958 classification system, is allocated to M.I.H. 872, in Professional and Scientific Services, S.I.C. Order XXII.

In conclusion, it has been estimated from the regional income and employment multiplier models used in this chapter that the effect of the University will be to increase the income level of the Study Area by between £3·93 millions and £4·88 millions by 1976 and between £6·5 millions and £8 millions by 1981, all at constant 1969/70 prices. The effect on employment will be to add a total of between 2,580 to 3,420 jobs to the local economy and a total of 4,300 to 5,800 jobs by 1981.

Table 7.1

Estimate of Wages and Salaries Component of J_2 for 1976

Staff	*Estimated staff numbers*	*Estimated average wage/ salary*	*Estimated total wage/ salary* (£'000)
Academic	439	£2,328	1,022
Departmental	229	1,182	271
Administration	126	1,372	173
Library	59	1,435	85
Others	516	771	398
	1,369		1,949

Table 7.2

Estimates of Students' Income for 1976

Students	*Numbers*	*Net Income from grant 1975–76 (per student)*	*Total net student income* (£'000)
Undergraduates			
University residents	2,300	266	611·8
Private lodgings	446	364	162·3
Home:			
within Study Area	343	294	100·8
outside Study Area	343	221	75·8
Postgraduates			
University residents	247	360	88·9
Private lodgings	49	550	27·0
Home:			
within Study Area	36	550	19·8
outside Study Area	36	413	14·9
	3,800		1,101·3
Balance of Vacation earnings (per student) £25			95·0
			1,196·3

Table 7.3

Estimates of Earnings of Immigrants for 1976

	Estimated net income (£M)	*Estimated share for 1975–76 immigrants* %	*Estimated* ΔZ *for 1975–76* £
Students	0·835	10·6	88,510
Staff			
Academic	·990	11·1	109,890
Departmental	·255	7·2	18,360
Administration	·164	6·7	10,988
Library	·081	8·9	7,209
Others	·386	2·1	8,106
			£243,063

Table 7.4

The Value of the Terms in the Model for 1976

J_1	£1·25 millions
J_2	£2·71 millions
ΔZ	£0·243 millions
k_r (lower)	1·24
k_r (upper)	1·54
m^*	0·75
n	2·43
z	0·09
ΔY (lower)	£3·93 millions (at 1969/70 prices)
ΔY (upper)	£4·88 millions (at 1969/70 prices)

Table 7.5

Estimated Breakdown of Employment Effect for 1976

S.I.C. order	*Lower case (persons)*	%	*Lower case (persons)*	%
III. Food, Drink and Tobacco	27	1	52	2
XVII. Construction	382	15	449	13
XVIII. Gas, Electricity and Water	27	1	52	2
XIX. Transport and Communication	18	1	35	1
XX. Distributive Trades	477	18	922	27
XXII. Professional and Scientific	1,370	53	1,370	40
XXIII. Miscellaneous Services	135	5	262	8
XXIV. Public Administration	144	6	278	8
	2,580		3,420	

APPENDIX A

Estimation of Indirect Employment (1976)

Estimates of indirect employment generated by the University were made by using the Greig employment multiplier model, as modified to provide lower and upper case values. The basic formulation developed by Greig was that

$$\Delta E_i = E_d\theta + \frac{\Delta V}{l}(1+0) + \frac{E_d w_d (k_a - 1)(k_b - 1)}{l(1-\theta_1) + w_p\theta_1} \qquad (23)$$

where the various items are defined in the table to this Appendix.

To use the model to obtain a lower case estimate of indirect employment to correspond to the lower case income estimate derived from using the Brown value for k_r, then the link between income and employment in public services must be eliminated.[30] This involves discarding the ratios θ and θ_1 and also w_p. Secondly, it is more convenient to use a modified formulation for ΔV, working from the Greig identities so that

$$\Delta V = E_d w_d (1 - s - t)(1 - m) \qquad (24)$$

Thus, by substitution and rearrangement

$$\Delta E_i = \frac{E_d w_d (1 - s - t)(1 - m) + (k_a - 1)(k_b - 1)}{l} \qquad (23')$$

The values for the various items in the employment multiplier are given in the table to this Appendix. Using these figures and the modified lower case Greig multiplier, it can be estimated that indirect employment generated by the University by 1976 will be 904 persons in the lower case.

The upper case income estimate made earlier was based on the Greig value for k_r so that, in the context of employment, the full Greig formulation, with its additional boost from public sector employment, will be used. Here, again, however, some modifications are necessary. Firstly, Greig estimates public sector employment as a ratio (θ) of direct employment and additional employment in the private sector. Direct employment, as defined for the University model, includes University staff, local resident construction workers, and students. This direct employment differs in nature from the E_d figure used by Greig, in that the students have a much lower level of expenditure, a much smaller household size background than the typical direct employee, and normally use public service facilities for only part of the year. If a rough, income-equivalent approach is taken to weight for these lower expenditure and household demands, and it is assumed that four

[30] Since the boosting effect of this relationship is not included in the Brown formulation.

students are the equivalent of one normal direct employee[31] as regards demand on public services, then a modified figure for direct employment (E'_d) can be estimated. Secondly, the Greig formulation that $\Delta V = E_d w_d v$ is used. The modified multiplier for the upper case will then read

$$\Delta E_i = E'_d\theta + \frac{E_d w_d v}{l}(1+\theta) + \frac{E_d w_d (k_a - 1)(k_b - 1)}{l(1-\theta_1) + w_p\theta_1} \qquad (23'')$$

The upper case values for this multiplier are also given in the table to this Appendix. From these values, it can be estimated that, in the upper case, there will be an additional 1,742 jobs in direct employment generated by the University in 1976.

Table (a) *Values for Greig Employment Multiplier*

		Lower case	*Upper case*
E_d	=direct employment	5,353	—
w_d	=wages of E_d	£548	—
$E_d w_d$	=income of direct employees	£2·93m.	£2·94m.
s	=average propensity to save	0·06	—
t	=average propensity to tax	0·18	—
m	=average propensity to import	0·71	—
k_a	=first rounds multiplier	1·35	1·40
k_b	=second and other rounds multiplier	1·25	1·35
l	=income needed to create an additional job	£1,000	£850
E'_d	=modified direct employees	—	2,503
θ	=ratio of public service to other employees	—	0·156
ΔV	=additional local value added from expenditure of direct employees' incomes	—	£646,000
θ_1	=ration of public service : total employment	—	0·156
w_p	=average wage in public service	—	£950
ΔE_i	=indirect employment generated	904	1,742

APPENDIX B

Industrial Structure of the Indirect Employment

The two basic assumptions made here are that, firstly, the pattern of indirect employment generated will follow the expenditure pattern of University incomes and, secondly, that this expenditure pattern will be similar to that estimated for Scotland as a whole over the period 1967–69, as given by the

[31] Average income per student, £400; average income per direct employee, about £1,600. A similar type of export base approach taken by Cooke (*Annals of Regional Science*, Vol. 4, June 1970) was that three students would be the equivalent of one direct employee. This lower ratio would add 50 jobs to indirect employment if it was used.

Family Expenditure Survey.[32] Both of these assumptions are rather sweeping. In particular the similarity of indirect employment and expenditure patterns will only occur if further assumptions are made that capacity in all expenditure sections is already fully utilised and that the relationship between employment, productivity and expenditure is the same for all sections, i.e. £x of expenditure in any section will give rise to the employment of one additional person.

The method used was to take the summary pattern of Scottish weekly household expenditure; since there was no detailed breakdown of these figures available, they were allocated into sub-groups within the expenditure categories as for the U.K. This made possible a more detailed, if still rough, examination of the categories, partly to make allowance for local industry supplies of goods and partly to allow a translation of the expenditure categories into S.I.C. Orders on the basis of M.L.H. definitions.

The table to this Appendix gives the result of the analysis. As could have been anticipated the bulk of expenditure items in all categories merely fall within the M.L.H. definitions of Order XX, Distributive Trades; however, the exercise does allow the identification of expenditure on important items such as car sales, part sales and services, i.e. Order XXIII, with minor other items such as Transport, Public Utilities and Food etc. A fairly high estimate for Construction (Order XVII) has been given on the grounds that the bulk of the housing for University immigrants is anticipated to be private and, where local authority housing is provided, this will tend to be in addition to local requirements; thus, both sections will tend to represent new construction rather than maintenance activity. Finally, in column 2, it is assumed that the Greig figure for public service employment of about 16% of the total will apply to the indirect employment generated; the F.E.S. figures are then adjusted to allow for this.

Table (a)

Estimated Breakdown of Indirect Employment for 1976

		Expenditure 1967–69	*Indirect employment 1975–76*
		%	%
III.	Food, Drink and Tobacco	3·2	3
XVII.	Construction	9·3	8
XVIII.	Gas, Electricity and Water	4·0	3
XIX.	Transport and Communications	1·9	2
XX.	Distributive Trades	63·6	53
XXIII.	Miscellaneous Services	18·0	15
XXIV.	Public Administration and Defence		16
			100

[32] See Table 17, F.E.S., Regional section.

8

The Impact of the New Project on Local Population

The previous chapter provided estimates of the impact on local incomes and employment. The purpose of this chapter is to provide the final series of estimates on the impact of the project on local population. It is probable that this last aspect of impact will be of the most direct interest to physical planners.

Here again, the necessary estimates can be based on the data provided in the earlier chapters. The impact of the project on population will depend ultimately on the immigrants brought to the area by either the direct or indirect employment associated with the project. The first step in estimating population impact must therefore involve an analysis of the nature of both direct and secondary growth, or indirect, employment, so that the immigrant proportions of each category can be identified.

Two main problems must be recognised here. Firstly, in direct employment the reliance on immigrants for staffing will tend to vary considerably between the different grades of staff. Typically, appointment to senior and the more highly skilled posts will be more dependent on outsiders rather than local residents, with reliance on the latter being more common for the less senior and skilled posts. The actual proportions will obviously depend on the extent and depth on the local labour market for the area and on the possibility of commuting from adjoining labour markets. Secondly, the nature of the indirect employment generated by the project will also influence the immigrant proportion of this category. Normally, unless there are strong manufacturing industry linkages, secondary growth employment will tend to be in the Service industry sector.[1] If this is the case, then Services employment will tend to be mainly for females. While families will move to the area for male employment, it is less likely that they will move for female employment. More normally, the female component of indirect employment will be made up from females resident in the area ,or female dependants of male immigrants to the area; if the latter, care must be taken not to double-count such females. It is therefore likely that the immigrant proportion of indirect employment will be rather lower than might at first seem to be the case – a

[1] See, for example, Table 7.5, page 88, and the relevant section on the Nature of The Additional Employment, in Chapter 7.

fact often missed in working papers on impact studies.[2]

Next, having estimated the immigrant proportions and computed the total number of immigrants to direct and indirect employment, further estimates must be made of the number of adult and child dependents which will be brought with immigrant employees to the area. The number of dependents will be governed by the age structure of the immigrant employees, which will influence the proportion of immigrants married and the family size of immigrant households. Again a common mistake[2] is to assume that immigrants will bring completed families with them into the area. Given the normal bias of migration flows towards the younger age groups,[3] this is rather unlikely; only a small proportion of migrants will have completed families, so that the child dependant ratio will tend to be fairly low.

As in all the estimates so far, the patterns selected for immigrant proportions and dependants ratios is essentially a matter of judgement, to be based on the nature of each individual project. The rest of this chapter merely illustrates how, for the Stirling case study, the proportions and ratios were derived and the final estimates made of the impact of the University of Stirling on the local population for 1976 and 1981.

The Impact of the University on Population

The impact of the University on the population of the Study Area will depend on the number of immigrants to the area who will be associated with the development of the University. The immigrants who will form the basis of the population effect of the University will consist of non-local students, academic, administrative and other directly employed staff, plus immigrants to the area for employment in the jobs generated in the secondary growth industries as a result of the University. The final immigrant population will be made up of these persons plus their dependants.

One way of estimating these numbers would be to use a questionnaire of staff and students to establish the patterns of age, sex, married proportions and family size, then take this as a 1970/71 population base for the population projection model developed in Chapter 4, to project for 1976 and 1981; assumptions of the timing of growth in numbers of students, staff and dependents, could be incorporated as the migration inflow data. This approach was not taken since, firstly, the existing age structure of students and staff are badly distorted towards the younger age groups[4] and would not provide

[2] In several of the physical planning papers concerned with the new Universities in the U.K., it has been taken that all, or nearly all indirect employment will be taken from immigrant sources, and that the child dependency ratio will reflect completed families, at the time of entry to the area.

[3] See Chapter 4, Appendix B, Table (*c*), page 43.

[4] The current age structure for students is distorted by the build-up from small initial intakes of 1967/68 and 1968/69, followed by the larger Phase II intakes of 1970/71 onwards.

a satisfactory population base and, secondly, the timing of the questionnaire, during the period of settlement into the new permanent buildings, would have caused a great deal of inconvenience, no matter how simply the form was constructed.

Accordingly, the approach adopted was to take the population age structure and sex figures as being the same as the pattern for Scottish Universities as a whole, with dependents also calculated from average Scottish figures, as estimated by the Registrar-General for Scotland, or as shown in the Sample Census of 1966, for Scotland. Since, over the period of its growth, the new University will 'age' towards the average pattern for all Scottish universities, the method is fairly defensible.

Estimates of Immigrant Students, Direct Staff and their Dependants for 1976

The figures for undergraduate and postgraduate students have been taken from the Development Plan.[5] From these figures have been deducted the estimated number of students already resident in the area, to provide final estimated figure for students immigrant to the Study Area in 1976 of 3,260 undergraduates and 350 postgraduates. If the age and sex distribution of these follows the Scottish pattern then it can be expected that 93% of undergraduates and about 51% of postgraduates will fall into the range 15–24, and that there will be 2,480 male and 1,130 female students.

The next stage is to provide estimates of the number of dependants brought into the Study Area by these immigrant students. In the absence of official statistics, local and S.E.D. grant sources suggest that about 10% of undergraduate and 50% of postgraduate students will be married. Making allowances for female students married to male students,[6] both at the University of Stirling, or married to persons already resident in the area, or to persons resident within commuting distance of the Study Area, it has been estimated that there will be 364 wives brought into the Study Area who have not been included in any other population estimate for 1976. Next, to estimate the number of child dependants of these married students, use has been made of Sample Census (1966) material on household composition by socio-economic group.[7] from this it has been estimated that there will be a further 350 child dependants, giving a total immigration population of about 4,300 students and dependants.

Next, the number of academic staff, covering all full-time teaching and

For staff, recruitment and senior appointments in the early years of the University have also resulted in a considerable divergence from the average pattern – University Court Papers.

[5] University of Stirling, Development Plan Report, 1968, Appendix C.

[6] These female students have been counted as immigrant dependants rather than separately as immigrant students.

[7] Sample Census, 1966, Household Composition Tables, Table 23, p. 80.

research personnel, has been estimated earlier[8] as 439 persons by 1976; if these follow the average sex pattern for all universities, 90% will be male staff and 10% female staff. All staff will be immigrants to the area. To provide estimates of the number of dependants it has been assumed that female staff will either be married to male staff (academic or other) or will be single and have no dependants. Hence adult dependants will be wives of married male staff; to obtain figures for these, it has been assumed that there will be the same proportion of married males per age group as for all professional employees in Scotland.[9] With the resultant figure of 321 married households in academic staff, again, given the professional employee pattern, it has been estimated that there will be 603 child dependants, 309 male and 294 female. Thus, with the 426 staff[10] there will be a population in 1976 of about 920 dependants. Even taking the slightly older age pattern for all Scottish universities, this immigrant population section will be relatively young; about 80% of this population will be aged under 40.

Non-academic staff have been estimated in two components: firstly, effectively non-manual workers, i.e. departmental, administrative and library staff, where there is a fair proportion of immigrants; secondly, estimates have been made for all other directly employed staff, effectively manual workers, i.e. work staff, maintenance, porters, groundsmen, cleaners and caterers, where there is a rather smaller proportion of immigrants. Of the original estimated total[11] of 930 staff in these various grades, it has been estimated that only 98 male and 167 female staff, a total of 265, will be immigrant to the area and therefore be part of the impact of the University on local population. It has been estimated that there will be a further 170 dependents of these employees, consisting of 79 wives and 91 children.

Thus the total immigrant population in 1976 of students, direct staff and dependents can be estimated at about 6,100, consisting of about 4,300 staff and students and about 1,800 dependants, 1,000 of these being children.

Estimates of Population from Secondary Growth by 1976

To complete the estimates for population impact, the immigrant population attributable to the growth of secondary employment generated by the University must be calculated. Two figures for secondary employment have been estimated earlier,[12] giving a range from a lower to an upper case. The lower case estimate was based on a low value for the regional income multiplier and a high value for the necessary amount of L.V.A. needed to create an additional

[8] See Table 7.1, page 87.
[9] *Annual Report of the Registrar-General of Scotland*, 1969, p. 29, table N.2.2.
[10] The shortfall is due to the exclusion of married female staff, who will appear as dependants here, or elsewhere.
[11] See Table 7.1, p. 87. [12] Chapter 7, 'Effect of the University on Local Employment.'

job. The upper case estimate was based on a higher value for the regional multiplier and a lower ratio of L.V.A.: employment creation. It was estimated that the figures for secondary growth employment generation would lie between the 900 of the lower case and the 1,740 of the upper case for 1976.

The first step in making the estimates for this chapter was to make allowance for the employment of any persons already resident in the Study Area, on the grounds that the direct impact of the University would be measured in terms of additional immigrants to the area. Then, on the basis of male/female proportions in the S.I.C. order structure of this type of employment,[13] it was estimated that 55% of the employment in secondary growth industries would be for males and 45% for females. It was then assumed than no female employees would be immigrants to the Study Area in their own right; they would be recruited from persons already immigrant to the Study Area, e.g. as dependents of other employees, or persons already resident in the Study Area, or would be commuters from outside the Study Area boundaries. The basis of the assumption is that no family will move to the Study Area purely for female employment.[14] On the other hand, it was assumed that all male employment in the secondary growth will be filled by immigrants, or by residents who would have to be replaced elsewhere by immigrants.[14] From these assumptions, it has been estimated that there will be between 492 and 949 immigrant employees in the lower and upper cases, respectively. If it is then taken that these males will be aged between 20–64 and that, within this range, they will have the same age structure as is typical for Scottish migrants, then estimates can be made of adult dependants, and, in turn, the number and age/sex structure of child dependants. In the lower case it was estimated that there would be 361 adult and 240 child dependants; in the upper case, this will be 695 adult and 467 child dependants.

Now all the various components of immigration population to the Study Area as a result of the establishment of the University, have been estimated. By 1976, it has been estimated that immigrants to direct employment and study at the University will amount to about 4,300 and that these will add to the local population a further 1,800 of their dependents. Further immigrants to the Study Area as a result of the jobs generated by the University in indirect employment have been estimated to number between 500 and 950 persons, who will bring with them between 500 and 900 dependants. In total, it has been estimated that the existence of the University will add, by 1976, between 7200 and 8,200 persons to the population of the Study Area.[15]

[13] See Table 7.5, page 88.

[14] Both assumptions are obviously rather extreme. There may be some component of widowed/divorced women with families. Equally, there may well be some recruitment to secondary growth employment of unemployed males (in view of the findings of Chapter 3 on the industrial structure and duration of unemployment, this will tend to be a very minor influence). In total numbers, there will tend to be some effect, but in age and sex structure there will be only minor inaccuracies added as a result of the assumptions.

[15] See Table 8.1, page 97.

Finally, the estimated age and sex structure of this new immigrant population is given in Table 8.2; about 90% of the population in both lower and upper cases is under 40 years of age. The largest proportion, due to the influence of the student population, is in the 10-year age range of 15–24 (effectively 18–24), which accounts for between 43% and 48%, of the immigrants. Again, in 1976, since the immigration has been to study and employment, there is no population component aged 65 and over.

The University's Impact on Population by 1981

It is necessary to make some estimate of the impact of the University on the local population by the completion of its growth towards its equilibrium size for Phase 3. By 1981, the immigrant population directly attributable to the University will consist of the earlier staff and indirect employment immigrants for 1976, adjusted for deaths and births over the quiquennium, plus new immigrants to employment at the University and secondary growth industries, plus the new, larger body of students and their dependants.

Applying the model developed for population projection of the Study Area population to the 1976 immigrant population, the assuming a continuation of the same type of pattern for age sex structure, marriage and family size for students and new employees at the University and secondary growth industries, provides estimates that, by 1981, the population impact from the University will amount to between 14,500 and 16,500. Over the period 1976–81 it has been estimated[16] that the normal increase in family size of the earlier immigrants will increase slightly the relative size of the 0–14 age group; equally, there will be a slight movement onwards through the age structure which will increase slightly the relative size of the 40–60 age group. Nevertheless, the main impact remains in the mid 15–39 group, which will still account for about 66% to 68% of the total, or 12,500 to 14,000 persons.

[16] See Table 8.3.

Table 8.1

Estimated Impact of the University on Population (1976)

	Lower case			*Upper case*		
	Male	*Female*	*Total*	*Female*	*Male*	*Total*
'Direct Employment'						
Students and staff	2,974	1,327	4,301	2,974	1,327	4,301
Dependants:						
Adult		764	764		764	764
Child	535	509	1,044	535	509	1,044
	3,509	2,600	6,109	3,509	2,600	6,109

Table 8.1 (contd.)

	Lower case			*Upper case*		
	Male	*Female*	*Total*	*Male*	*Female*	*Total*
'*Indirect Employment*'						
Employees	492		492	949		949
Dependants:						
Adult		361	361		695	695
Child	124	116	240	239	228	467
Overall total	4,125	3,077	7,202	4,697	3,523	8,220

Table 8.2

Total Immigrant Population for 1976

	Lower case				*Upper case*			
Age	*Male*	*Female*	*Total*	%	*Male*	*Female*	*Total*	%
0–4	253	230	483	6·7	288	271	559	6·8
5–9	259	245	504	7·0	304	288	592	7·2
10–4	151	144	295	4·1	181	172	353	4·3
15–9	821	555	1,376	19·1	822	560	1,382	16·8
20–4	1,392	666	2,058	28·5	1,492	686	2,178	26·5
25–9	411	324	735	10·2	501	403	904	11·0
30–4	266	267	533	7·4	370	353	723	8·8
35–9	187	216	403	5·6	247	263	510	6·2
40–4	158	195	353	4·9	197	247	444	5·4
45–9	86	94	180	2·5	123	115	238	2·9
50–4	72	72	144	2·0	90	83	173	2·1
55–9	65	65	130	1·8	74	74	148	1·8
60–4	4	4	8	0·1	8	8	16	0·2
	4,125	3,077	7,202		4,697	3,523	8,220	

Table 8.3

Estimate of Total Population Impact by 1981

	Lower case		*Upper case*	
	Persons	%	*Persons*	%
0–14	2,672	18·6	3,182	19·2
15–39	9,831	68·3	10,984	66·2
40–64	1,889	13·1	2,419	14·6
	14,392		16,585	

9

Overall Growth in the Study Area

The previous chapter completed the last of the series of estimates needed to provide a basis upon which policy measures might be formulated. All that remains to be done is to amalgamate all the estimates made for internal growth of the Study Area and the growth associated with the development of the new project. The methods by which projections could be made of internal growth in population and employment were discussed in Chapters 4 and 5, and illustrated with the Stirling case study figures. Equally, the methods by which the contribution of the new project to growth in income, employment and population could be analysed, were discussed in Chapters 6, 7 and 8, and were again demonstrated with reference to the new University of Stirling. The purpose of this chapter is to gather together the two series of estimates and examine their broad implications for the local area.

The Estimates for Population

In Chapter 4, it was estimated that, for 1976, population would grow internally, i.e. independently of University influences, from its base of 92,905 persons in 1961 to between 100,911 and 111,770 persons by the end of the period, depending on the assumptions made about the direction and volume of the net migration flow over the period.[1] For the 1981 target year, it was estimated that population would continue to grow to some total within the range of 103,330 to 118,485 persons.[1] The second component of population growth over the period, the population attracted to the area by University development and its related secondary growth forces, was estimated in the previous chapter to lie between 7,202 persons in the lower case and 8,220 persons in the upper case, by 1976.[2] For the later year of 1981, the University population component was estimated to lie between the range of 14,392 persons in the lower case and 16,585 persons in the upper case.[3]

Given the internal projections for the Stirling Study Area, the effect of including the University component is to raise the population estimates by a further 7% in the lower and 8% in the upper case for 1976. Depending upon the assumptions on migration patterns and the level of employment generated by the University, the amalgamated estimates predict a total population of

[1] See Table 4.1, p. 32. [2] See Table 8.1, p. 97. [3] See Table 8.3, p. 98.

between 108,000 and 120,000 persons for this year,[4] an increase of between 16·4% and 29·2% from its 1961 base figure. Since 70% of the University population component lies in the age group 15–39, as against the 33% in the age group at the time of the 1961 Census, the amalgamated projections indicate an increase in the size of this key reproduction group to between 37% and 38% of total population. The effect of this concentration of University population also reduces slightly the relative size of the other age groups as estimated for internal growth.[5]

For 1981, adding the University population range to the internal projections has the effect of increasing these by a further 15% in the lower and 18% in the upper case. Again depending an assumptions of migration pattern and the size of the employment multiplier, this provides a range of population estimates of between 118,000 and 135,000 persons for this later year,[6] representing an increase of between 26·7% and 45·4% on the 1961 base population. By this year, some marginal ageing will have taken place in the University population component, so that about 68% of this will lie in the 15–39 age group; nevertheless, combined internal and University growth forces suggest that this key group will have increased to a little over 40% of the total population by 1981 (against its 33% share for 1961).

The size and nature of such a population increase could have far reaching effects on both private and public sectors of the local economy. The private sector has already received, and will continue to receive a considerable increase in turnover, concentrated on the goods and services demanded by a larger, younger population, many of whom are just starting to establish houses and families. County planning officials have already made a series of studies and revisions for this upsurge in population, as it is currently being experienced, and its insistent pressures of spatial demands, for private house construction, retail distribution outlets and other types of services. They have already identified rapid growth in the predictable sectors concerned with house construction and sales, house furnishing, car sales and servicing, entertainments, bookstores, supermarkets, etc. In the public sector, the same pressures, and the expectation of even more severe pressures in the future, have triggered off a high level of activity in the improvement of existing capacity and the provision of additional capacity in services for education, hospitals, maternity, housing and roads.

The Estimates for Employers

Looking next at the overall situation in employment, it was estimated in Chapter 5 that the employment offered in local workplaces would increase

[4] See Table 9.1; since the objective here is to indicate a range within which population might fall, Projection II, the zero migration case, has been ignored.

[5] See Table 4.2, page 33.

[6] See Table 9.2, page 103.

from its base total of 37,400 jobs in 1961 to 39,650 jobs in 1976, and 41,050 jobs by 1981, as a result of purely internal growth forces.[7] It was also observed that, inherent in this growth, would be marked changes in the local industrial structure, with the fast expanding Services sector causing a swing away from the older Manufacturing and Primary industry base. From the University component, on the other hand, it is estimated that by 1976 a further 2,580 to 3,420 jobs will be provided, about 1,400 of these in direct and the balance in indirect employment.[8] Here too, the industrial composition of this employment is markedly different from the established pattern of employment and this will accelerate the swing away from the older industrial base.[9] For 1981, the additional jobs stemming from University development and its secondary growth will total between 4,300 and 5,800 (about 2,700 of this in University employment of various kinds). This larger total will have similar industrial characteristics to the 1976 figures.

Amalgamating both growth sources has the effect of raising the projected rate of internal increase of about 6% for the period 1961–76 to about 13% in the lower and 15% in the upper case. By 1976 therefore, the development of the new University should at least double the rate of growth in employment which could reasonably have been expected.

The impact of the University, while it does not alter greatly the projected ranking of the main industries, does tend to exaggerate and confirm the importance of the growth sectors.[10] Professional and Scientific Services, under the impetus of both internal and University growth, rises from the 5th largest industry in 1961, with about 3,000 employees, to be the largest industry by 1976, with about 6,300 employees. Another industry affected by both sources of growth is Distributive Trades, rising from 3rd largest, with about 3,600 employees in 1961, to be second largest, with between 4,700 and 5,200 employees in 1976. Construction, 6th largest in 1961, ruses to 3rd largest, with over 4,000 employees in 1976. The other main industries affected by University growth, although to a much lesser extent, are Public Administration and Miscellaneous Services; the effect on other S.I.C. Orders is insignificant.

The combined figures for 1981 are presented only in the broad industrial categories, in view of the various problems associated with longer term employment forecasts.[11] The changes observed for 1976 continue, with Primary and Manufacturing industry categories declining in relative size so that they ultimately provide only between 36% and 37% of total employment, as opposed to over 50% in the base year 1961. Construction, it has been estimated, will continue to develop steadily to employ about 12% of the total

[6] See Table 9.2, p. 103. [7] See Table 5.2, p. 51. [8] See Table 7.5, p. 88.
[9] See Table 3.1, p. 24 and Chapter 3, section on The Pattern of Industry.
[10] See Table 9.3, p. 104.
[11] See Table 9.4, p. 104; the forecasting problems are discussed in Chapter 5.

labour force. The main result of the various projections has been to show a fairly massive expansion of employment in the Services sector, taking it from its initial 39% to between 50% and 52% of total employment by the end of the period, an increase of 61% in jobs offered by this group of industries.

The estimated effect of the two sources of growth has been to cause a considerable shift from the older, traditional sources of employment to a new employment structure where one job in every two will be in the Services sector. This will, by no means, be the effect of every new project. For other manufacturing industry types of new project, the boost given to Services employment is liable to be rather less, partly because it has been exaggerated in the Stirling case study by the direct employment in the project itself (University employment is Service industry employment), and partly because a new manufacturing development is more likely to stimulate some internal manufacturing trade flows as well as Services employment.

To conclude, therefore, in the Stirling case study it can be seen that the introduction of a major new project into a relatively prosperous sub-region[12] has contributed strongly towards the considerable expansion in population and employment in that local economy. Indeed, in the following chapter it is argued that the ultimate effects on both employment and population could well be even greater than estimated here. However, given the magnitude of these changes estimated, it is inevitable that considerable strains will be imposed on the local labour market[13] and the labour markets in adjoining areas, and on all aspects of spatial planning for industrial, servicing and recreational land use in the local area. The provision of joint estimates in the form of this chapter should provide some scientific basis of fact and projection upon which any necessary public policies can be formulated.

[12] In Chapters 2 and 3, analysis showed that, prior to the establishment of the University, the sub-region has fared better in population and employment terms than the Scottish average.

[13] Comparison of the various projections for population and employment indicate that there seems to be a marginal decline in the area's Activity Rate over the period. There are two reasons why this should be so: firstly, much of the internal growth in population reflects the current commuter inflow (employment of these persons cannot be registered as local employment); secondly, a fair proportion of the University population consists of students, who, as a result of their much lower incomes and part-year residence, will generate less employment than normal full-time direct employees. Any such decline in the local Activity Rate should not be interpreted as a lower level of economic activity.

Table 9.1 *Estimated Total Population of the Study Area (1976)*

(a) Lower case

	1961		*1976*			
			Projection I		*Projection III*	
Age	*Persons*	%	*Persons*	%	*Persons*	%
0–14	25,445	27·4	28,434	26·3	31,409	26·4
15–39	30,614	33·0	40,326	37·3	44,733	37·6
40–64	27,603	29·7	27,136	25·1	30,457	25·6
65 and over	9,243	9·9	12,217	11·3	12,373	10·4
	92,905		108,113		118,972	

(b) Upper case

	1976			
	Projection I		*Projection III*	
	Persons	%	*Persons*	%
0–14	28,701	26·3	31,558	26·3
15–39	40,924	37·5	45,236	37·7
40–64	27,283	25·0	30,717	25·6
65 and over	12,223	11·2	12,479	10·4
	109,131		119,990	

Table 9.2 *Estimated Total Population of the Study Area (1981)*

(a) Lower case

	1961		*1981*			
			Projection I		*Projection III*	
Age	*Persons*	%	*Persons*	%	*Persons*	%
0–14	25,445	27·4	30,308	25·7	34,497	26·0
15–39	30,614	33·0	47,964	40·7	53,439	40·2
40–64	27,603	29·7	26,740	22·7	31,822	23·9
65 and over	9,243	9·9	12,710	10·8	13,119	9·9
	92,905		117,722		132,877	

(b) Upper case

	1981			
	Projection I		*Projection III*	
Age	*Persons*	%	*Persons*	%
0–14	30,818	25·7	35,007	25·9
15–39	49,117	41·0	54,592	40·4
40–64	27,264	22·7	32,346	23·9
65 and over	12,716	10·6	13,125	9·7
	119,915		135,070	

Table 9.3

Projected Total Employment Structure (1976)

	1961		*1976 Lower*		*1976 Upper*	
	Persons	%	*Persons*	%	*Persons*	%
II. Mining	5,044	13·5	3,250	7·7	3,250	7·6
X. Textiles	4,346	11·6	3,950	9·4	3,950	9·2
XX. Distributive Trades	3,612	9·7	4,727	11·2	5,172	12·0
XXIII. Miscellaneous Services	3,138	8·4	3,585	8·5	3,712	8·6
XX. Professional and Scientific	2,995	8·0	6,270	14·9	6,270	14·6
XVII. Construction	2,899	7·7	4,032	9·6	4,099	9·5
XXIV. Public Administration	2,652	7·1	2,794	6·6	2,928	6·8
III. Food, Drink and Tobacco	2,398	6·4	2,127	5·0	2,152	5·0
XIX. Transport	1,719	4·6	1,718	4·1	1,735	4·0
XV. Paper and Printing	1,569	4.2	1,700	4·0	1,700	4·0
VI. Engineering	1,503	4·0	1,700	4·0	1,700	4·0
XIII. Bricks, Potteries and Glass	1,340	3·6	1,750	4·2	1,750	4·1
All Other Orders	4,198	11·2	4,527	10·7	4,552	10·6
Total	37,413		42,130		42,970	

Table 9.4

Estimates of Total Employment for 1981

	1961		*1981 Lower*		*1981 Upper*	
	Persons	%	*Persons*	%	*Persons*	%
Primary	5,725	15·3	3,700	8·2	3,700	7·9
Manufacturing	13,291	35·5	13,207	29·2	13,252	28·4
Construction etc.	3,779	10·1	5,517	12·2	5,682	12·2
Services	14,618	39·1	22,811	50·4	24,101	51·6
	37,413		45,235		46,735	

10

Conclusions

Throughout the book, there have been two main objectives. The first of these has been to provide estimates of the economic impact of a new University on its local economy. The second objective has been to show that the various techniques used in this study are capable of more general application; effectively, this has involved an explanation and generalisation of the methodology used to achieve the first objective. The differing emphasis of these two aspects of the book suggests that any conclusions must themselves be taken in the form of two sections.

The first section of this chapter is therefore concerned with the economic repercussions of the development of a new University. While the magnitude of these repercussions will be influenced by the nature of the local economy, at least as far as the secondary growth aspects are concerned, and while the rate of development of the University might well be constrained by the demands of other internal growth forces in the local economy, it is not intended to cover again the analysis of the local economy and the overall growth situation.[1] In this chapter, attention is focussed solely on the contribution from University growth, on its importance to the local economy, and on its possible implications for regional policy.

The second section is on the methodology of the regional income multiplier approach and is divorced from the results of the Stirling case study. Its purpose is to review the main advantages of the approach, examine the basic logic behind the method, outline the broad steps by which the series of estimates can be made, and to examine some of the major problems associated with the regional income multiplier approach.

The Economic Impact of a New University

By 1976 the University will add per annum, from construction expenditure on the campus, earnings of staff and students and other investment induced locally to support its development, between £3·93 millions and £4·88 millions,

[1] For an analysis of the main features of the local economy see Chapters 2 and 3; the forecasts for internal growth are in Chapters 4 and 5; the combined effect of internal and University growth is discussed in Chapter 9.

H

at 1969/70 constant prices, to the income level of the Study Area economy. By 1981, even allowing for the completion of construction work on the campus and on capacity extensions elsewhere, the University will still add an estimated £6·5 millions to £8·0 millions to local income, again at 1969/70 prices.

The University impact figures for employment generation, based as they are partly on the income estimates made above and partly on the assumption of different ratios for income: employment generation, have also been estimated as a range. It has been estimated that the total of all forms of employment associated with the development of the University would amount to, by 1976, between 2,580 and 3,420 jobs. By 1981, even with the completion of the construction work on the campus, it has been estimated that there will be between 4,300 and 5,800 jobs. This was composed of, in 1976, employment at the University for about 1,680 persons, with between 900 and 1,740 persons employed indirectly; for 1981, direct employment at the University has been estimated at about 2,700 persons, with a further 1,600 to 3,100 persons employed in secondary growth.

Finally, the effect of the University on the population of the Study Area will depend upon the number of additional persons, i.e. non-residents, brought to the area to study or to employment, both direct and indirect, together with the dependants of all these. It has been estimated that, for 1976, there will be an immigrant population of about 4,300 students and staff and a further 1,800 dependants of these. With the estimates for immigrant indirect employees and their dependants, the overall additional population attributable to the University amounts to between 7,200 and 8,200 persons. For 1981, taking account of the increases in the family size of previous immigrants as well as the additional immigrants to study and employment, with their dependants, the total immigrant population attributable to the University has been estimated at between 14,500 and 16,500 persons.[2]

Returning to the original estimates of income generation, which provide the basis for part of the employment and therefore population estimates, it can be argued that the upper case multiplier value used of $k_r = 1{\cdot}54$ is likely to be more relevant to the situation in the Study Area than the lower case value of $k_r = 1{\cdot}24$. The explanation for this is that the upper case value was estimated from a model which was constructed specifically to deal with the income/employment interaction of the type of immigration situation likely to occur in the Study Area; the lower case value is based on a simple, conventional multiplier model which ignores immigration effects. Thus,

[2] If, as now seems likely, the University achieves its 'final size' at a year later than 1981, this will have only a marginal effect on the University estimates for this year (the population growth of the 1976 staff population will increase slightly the family size of those staff remaining with the University). It will, however, affect the estimates of overall growth given in Chapter 9. The strong internal growth forces identified in population and employment will have to be projected forward again to the new final size date. The overall totals will therefore be greater than estimated by virtue of continuing internal growth.

while its use to provide a lower case income figure can be justified, it is nevertheless likely that the actual income figure will tend to lie towards the upper end of the range estimated. If this is so, then the type of situation prevailing in the Stirling Study Area will tend to push the estimates for indirect and therefore total employment, in their turn, towards the upper end of the ranges estimated. Given the influence of the income estimates on employment, it can then be argued that the estimates for immigrant population to the University and secondary growth sectors will also tend to lie towards the upper end of the range estimated.

It is possible that the final effects of the growth of the University could exceed the estimates given above. As regards population, the area has in the past suffered a steady and significant net migration loss from the 18–30-year-old section of its indigenous population. The combined influences of a markedly younger University population and the cultural and recreational facilities set up around this on the campus and elsewhere might do something to stem this drain on the local population. Secondly, the same factors should continue to promote the development of the area as a desirable residential base for commuters. Thirdly, the University immigrant population, the retained emigrants from the indigenous population, and the commuter immigrants to the area are all, given the nature of migration flows, likely to be in the main reproductive age groups; this should continue to boost the rise in local birth rates, which can already be observed in many districts of the Study Area, and increase the rate of growth of population in the long term.[3]

The employment position is less clear. In the early years of the University, there were indications of strong and independent growth forces within the local economy. The effect of the University will be to at least double the projected internal rate of expansion – with the further problem that both sets of growth forces tend to be located in the Services sector. Apart from accelerating the swing away from the older, traditional industries, this raises the possibility that the two sets of growth forces might be competitive and impose severe constraints upon each other. Currently, there is no evidence of this. Apart from the obvious slack introduced to the male labour market in particular by the current nationwide recession, additional female jobs are being filled comfortably by local and immigrant dependent female labour. While the female expansion can reasonably expect to be staffed by the rising local female Activity Rates and the steady inflow of female dependants seeking employment, the acid test of conflicting growth forces is more likely to be felt in the male labour market, if the normal pattern of quick recovery

[3] This type of interaction between immigration and birth rates was illustrated in the Projection III model of Chapter 4. If the migration net inflow exceeds the value given to it in this model (and retained emigrants are the equivalent of new immigrants), then the rate of population growth wlli exceed even the Projection III rate.

from recession is repeated. One saving feature here might well be that University employment of local males has been confined largely to the lower skilled and unskilled posts, and is therefore unlikely to clash directly with local industrial expansion.

A further factor creating some uncertainty as to the future position in employment is the possibility of a third wave of development in the local area triggered off by some of the forces associated with the University. Research into the location decisions of firms suggests that unquantifiable factors, such as an atmosphere of growth and prosperity, or a desirable residential area, can weigh heavily in favour of an area in the decisions of firms seeking a new site. The growth of the University will undoubtedly cause a rapid expansion of population and of expenditure levels locally, and it is possible that some of its more cultural influences will augment the attractions of an already desirable area. In more formal terms, the rapid expansion forecast of population (representing a supply of labour) and Services sector facilities, could well generate sufficient agglomeration economies to attract further new firms to the area. The effects of this rapid interaction between population, income and employment can be observed in the remarkable rate of growth of sub-regions such as the nearby Falkirk/Grangemouth complex. At this stage, however, it is only conjecture that similar growth forces could be experienced in the local area around Stirling.

Either in terms of the estimates which have been given earlier, or the more arguable possibility of a third wave of development, it is clear that a new University should provide a massive boost to its local economy. While it will stimulate local manufacturing linkages rather less than a more industrial project might, its heavy reliance on immigrant staff and the resultant pressures from the expenditures of these and the students still have considerable repercussions on local incomes and employment.

This, in turn, suggests that the siting of a new University, or an equivalent educational establishment, affects more than merely the academic opportunities in a region. If the University of Stirling situation is typical, the establishment of a major educational centre can provide a significant amount of regional stimulation. The siting of such an educational establishment should therefore be considered more in terms of an act of regional policy than seems to have been the case in the past.

The Methodology of the Regional Income Multiplier Approach

The second main objective of the book has been to show how the regional multiplier approach offers a relatively simple but workable means of assessing quickly the main aspects of the economic impact of a new object. With the export-base approach apparently discredited in planning studies, despite some of its more attractive aspects, it would appear that most of the economic impact studies completed in recent years, or currently in progress, are based on regional input-output models. While the information gathered into such tables ultimately provides valuable data on regional and inter-regional industrial relationships for planners, this approach faces severe problems in connection with the selection of industries and the time and cost involved in processing the data gathered.[4] In many cases, the main economic questions involved could be answered by the type of multiplier model constructed in this book. The advantages offered by the latter approach are its more modest data requirements, and its relative simplicity and speed of operation.

Given these by no means unimportant advantages, its results do not differ widely from those achieved by using the alternative approaches. Taking the Stirling results, comparison of the final income figures to the initial injection values for 1976, yields an effective income multiplier of 1·45 in the lower case and 1·80 in the upper case. This compares with the implicit multiplier value of 1·85 derived by Blake and McDowall[5] from their input-output analysis of the contribution from the University of St Andrews to its local economy. Again for 1976, this is also true of the effective employment multiplier; the generation of between 900 and 1,740 jobs in secondary growth indicates an employment multiplier[6] of between 1·36 and 1·70. This compares to the export-base approaches of Cooke's[7] estimate of 1·4 for the University of Florida, and Weiss and Gooding's estimates of between 1·6 and 1·8 for defence installations in Portsmouth, New Hampshire.[8]

The actual process by which the regional multiplier approach can be adapted for use as an operational model by planners has been discussed in detail in the earlier chapters.[9] In outline, the first stage is to estimate the impact of the new project on local income levels. The main problem here is to distinguish between sources of income generation (the multiplicand) and the process of income generation (the multiplier). The nature and number of the sources of income generation will vary between projects. The essential thing is to formulate the multiplicand with care, so that it includes all the significant sources of income related to the project, stated net of all immediate leakages from the area. The net total of all these income sources for a given year makes up the multiplicand, or the initial injection. This must then be

[4] See Chapter 6.

[5] C. Blake and S. McDowall, 'A Local Input-Output Table', *Scottish Journal of Political Economy*, November 1967.

[6] The direct employment figure used here includes a 'direct employment equivalent' component for students. To ignore the latter would be to exaggerate the employment generation effects of genuine direct employees, and give a range of 1·53 and 2·03.

[7] E. Cooke, 'Analysing University Student Contribution to the Economic Base of the Community', *Annals of Regional Science*, June 1970.

[8] S. J. Weiss and E. C. Gooding, 'Estimation of Differential Employment Multipliers', *Land Economics*, No. 44, 1968.

[9] See Chapters 6, 7 and 8.

subjected to the multiplier process, i.e. the process by which income is generated during the various rounds of expenditure within the local community. To make allowance for the various factors which will influence the extent to which income is generated, such as the area's industrial structure, any unique characteristics in its expenditure, the flow of immigration, if any, stimulated by the project, it is suggested that a lower and upper range of multiplier values be used.[10]

The income multiplier model developed for the Stirling case study contains three main modifications to the conventional application of the model. Firstly, it suggests that the economic base used for the model should be a sub-region rather than the more normal standard region economy, on the grounds that the economic impact of most projects will be concentrated on the former; the effect of most projects may be quite marginal when measured against a standard region. While the use of a more local region may have direct benefits for planners, it might seem, at first sight, that the use of a smaller economic base will reduce the multiplier effects of the project. Normally the smaller the ecomonic base, the greater is the dependence of the sub-region on imported goods, i.e. the greater is the leakage from expenditure rounds. Nevertheless, it is this smaller economic base which should be used.

The second modification is to recognise the effects of immigration on the multiplier process. Basing the analysis on a sub-region increases the probability of immigration to the project, both from other standard regions and from other parts of the standard region in which the project is situated. Where a significant immigration flow results, then the effects of the volume and pattern of expenditure and the indirect employment generated by this necessitates the use of the Greig type of formulation. The conventional model, by missing the income/employment interactions of this situation, would understate the economic effects of the project in this type of situation.

The third modification was to recognise the effect of such an immigration inflow in the formulation of the multiplicand. The rising income and expenditure from the new project, coupled with the pressure of an additional population in the area, will place considerable strain on existing capacity in both private and public sectors of the local economy. These pressures are likely to induce capacity extensions in both sectors, so that there is no longer any justification for excluding this term from the multiplicand. Similarly, if other income sources can be identified, e.g. in the form of inter-industry linkages benefiting from the new project, the extent of this benefit should also be included in the multiplicand. In the Stirling case study, merely including values for construction expenditure and induced investment, in addition to the normal ongoing wages and salaries, increased the multiplied

[10] See Chapter 6, the section on the Generalisation of the Multiplier Model, for a discussion of these points and suggested values for the multiplier.

expansion of income by between 25% and 30%, with all its repercussions on indirect employment and population. This underlines how important it is to include all the relevant income components in the multiplicand.

Leaving the main analysis of the impact of the project on local incomes, the next main stage is to establish the figures for total employment attributable to the project. This employment will consist of both direct employment in the project and indirect employment generated in the secondary growth. It is for the latter type of employment that the income generation figures are essential. It is basically from these figures that indirect employment is calculated, either by the crude method of dividing the figure for additional income generated locally by some average income figure, or by the preferred method of using an employment multiplier approach, which estimates indirect employment from a combination of direct employment figures and income generated.

The final main stage is to analyse the figures for direct and indirect employment to establish, given the nature of the project and its secondary growth, the extent to which staffing needs are met from local and outside resources. The use of non-local labour will determine the number of immigrants brought to the area. These can then, on the basis of their age structure and socio-economic groupings, provide the data from which estimates can be made of adult and child dependants. The number of immigrants and their dependants represent the impact of the project on the local population.

By using these various steps, it is argued, the regional income multiplier model can be used as an operational tool for physical planning, as well as its more normal function of providing a theoretical base for the assessment of public policy measures. However, in common with the alternative measures of economic impact, it has inherent weaknesses in its empirical work, which must be fully recognised before any decisions are made on the basis of its results.

There are three main problem areas. Firstly, the model will operate smoothly only in a situation where capacity in the local economy is fairly well utilised, i.e. there is no significant degree of slack. In such a situation the generation of both additional employment for existing capacity and induced investment in capacity extension is likely. On the other hand, if the project is sited in an area where there exists a considerable degree of underutilised capacity in both labour and capital, then it becomes difficult to estimate clearly the full income and employment effects of the new project. Here it is likely that some, possibly most of the employment in the project will be taken from local labour, thus removing or reducing the inflow of immigrants to the area; in turn, the generation of additional indirect employment and induced investment seems less likely. In such a situation, the establishment of a new project might seem only to maintain existing employment, income, services and employment, without any improvement to the area. In fact there is a counter argument to this in that where employment is replaced and held, emigration from the sub-region is halted or reduced; the retention of a potential emigrant, in strict multiplier terms, is equivalent to the attraction of an immigrant, i.e. the income and employment effects of the project should be measured not merely against past levels where employment is replaced, but against the possible levels which would have resulted if the run-down had not been stopped or the spare capacity taken up. Both Archibald and Brown argue that such a run-down would be cumulative and considerable and there exists much prima facie evidence in Scotland to support this claim. Yet, while in theory the retention of indirect employment and capacity can be attributed to the project, in reality to what extent can this be quantified by the sub-regional model?

Secondly, there is the whole problem of timing in the multiplier process, an aspect of the analysis which seems to be, as yet, untouched in terms of publication. Even assuming a reasonable degree of capacity utilisation, it is difficult to estimate how quickly the various multiplier lags will operate and the income, expenditure, employment generation and income cycle be completed. Equally, in the multiplicand, it is difficult to estimate with certainty how quickly construction on the project and on induced investment will take effect on income levels, or for how long, after its completion, it will continue to influence incomes. In particular, where the project is relatively large, as at Fort William, or Stirling, or Invergordon, the prolonged and considerable activity in construction is likely to cause an expansion in the employment and size of many a construction or construction servicing firms locally; while, in theory, the completion of this work will cause lay-offs and the return to the previous 'equilibrium' levels, to what extent in reality might it not stimulate continuing growth in these firms, or at least the desire to hold the firms at their expanded size? And, finally, in relation to induced investment, how quickly will this be induced by expenditure pressures and to what extent will the decision to provide extended capacity and the time-path of its provision be undermined by 'queuing'? In a slack capacity situation, the problems of lagged response will multiply; equally, the difficulties in the assessment of the timing of the run-down and contraction in the region are obvious and considerable.

The third problem, one shared by all of the impact study methods, is that the multiplier model as shown assumes that its coefficients will remain stable over the period of the analysis. In reality, this is unlikely. The major changes which are likely to take place in the local industrial structure, or indeed the economy as a whole, will tend to affect the values attributed to coefficients both in the multiplier and the multiplicand. In particular, the various propensities to import might well change as the industrial structure broadens. Changes in productivity and technology might well disturb the various employment ratios. The capital:output ratio used for induced investment is open over a prolonged time period to all the problems of capacity, response, indivisibilities and technology changes inherent in the concept. If it is felt that instability in its coefficients will affect significantly the accuracy of its forecasts, then some attempt could be made to estimate the nature of these changes and incorporate them into a more dynamic version of the income multiplier model. In most cases, it may be sufficient to acknowledge the issue as a source of further inaccuracy in the estimates, rather than an obstacle to the estimates being made.

Despite all the problems involved, and it is repeated that any approach in impact studies has problems, it is suggested that these are outweighed by the relative simplicity of the regional income multiplier model. For many new projects, the results provided should be of sufficient accuracy for planning purposes. It is therefore hoped that the techniques used in the Stirling case study will provide genuine operational assistance to planners and others.

BIBLIOGRAPHY

This bibliography contains references to the works cited in the text of the thesis. Apart from these works, considerable use has been made of the statistics contained in various publications, such as the Census Returns for 1951, 1961 and 1966 for Scotland, the United Kingdom, the Scotland, County Reports and special volumes on Economic Activity, Household Composition, Migration, and Workplace; apart from these Census publications, extensive use has also been made of various issues of the *Department of Employment Gazette* (formerly the *D.E.P. Gazette* and the *M.O.L. Gazette*) and the Annual Reports of the Registrar-General for Scotland, both over the period 1951–70. In addition to these main sources of statistical data, further references have been made to the data contained in the various issues during this period of the *Abstract of Regional Statistics*, the *Digest of Scottish Statistics*, the *Family Expenditure Survey*, *National Income and Expenditure*, *Statistics of Education*, and *Statistics on Prices, Incomes and Productivity*. Finally, use has been made of unpublished statistical data from the Accounts Department of the University of Stirling, the Census Office, the Department of Employment, and the Registrar-General for Scotland.

Allen, K. J., 'The Regional Multiplier', chapter 4, *Regional and Urban Studies*, Department of Economic and Social Research, Glasgow University, 1969.

Allen, K. J. & Orr, S. C., 'Industry and Employment', chapter 4, *Grangemouth/Falkirk Regional Survey and Plan*, Vol. 1, Glasgow University, 1966.

Archibald, G. C., 'Regional Multiplier Effects in the U.K.', *Oxford Economic Papers*, March 1967.

Beckerman, W. & Associates, 'The British Economy in 1975', *National Institute of Economic and Social Research Studies*, No. 23, 1965.

Benjamin, B., *Demographic Analysis*, 1968.

Blake, C. & McDowall, S., 'A Local Input-Output Table', *Scottish Journal of Political Economy*, November 1967.

Brown, A. J., Lind, H. & Bowers, J., The 'Green Paper on Development Areas', *National Institute Economic Review*, No. 40, May 1967.

Central Statistical Office, *National Accounts Statistics: Sources and Methods*, Official Statistics, 13.

Cooke, E., 'Analysing University Student Contribution to the Economic Base of the Community', *Annals of Regional Science*, June 1970.

Cox, P. R., *Demography*, 3rd edition, 1966.

Czamanski, S., and Malizia, E. E., 'Applicability and Limitations of the Use of National Input-Output Tables for Regional Studies', *Regional Science Association Papers*, Vol. 23, 1969.

Department of Economic Affairs, *The National Plan*, 1965, Cmnd 2764.

Department of Economic Affairs, *The Task Ahead: Economic Assessment to 1972*, 1969.

Frieman Fox, Wilbur Smith & Associates, *Traffic Study Report*, 1967.

Grauman, J. V., *The Study of Population*, edited by P. M. Hauser and O. D. Duncan, 1968, chapter 23.

Greig, M. A., 'The Regional Income and Employment Effects of a Paper Mill', *Scottish Journal of Political Economy*, February 1971.

Greig, M. A., 'Regional Multiplier Effects in the U.K.: A Comment', *Oxford Economic Papers*, Vol. 23, No. 2, July 1971.

Greig, M. A., *The Economic Impact of the Highlands and Islands Development Board Investment in Fisheries*, 1972.

Godley, W. A. H. & Shepherd, J. R., 'Long-term Growth and Short-term Policy', *National Institute Economic Review*, August 1964.

Hughes, J. T., 'Edinburgh and the Lothians', chapter 10, *The Lothians Regional Survey and Plan*, Vol. 1, University of Glasgow, 1966.

Hughes, J. T., 'Employment Projections and Urban Development', chapter 9, *Regional and Urban Studies*, Department of Economic and Social Research, Glasgow University, 1969.

Hunt, A., *Government Social Survey: A Survey of Women's Employment*, 1968.

Ilersic, A. R., *Statistics*, 12th edition, 1963.

Isard, W., *Methods of Regional Analysis: An Introduction to Regional Science*, 1960.

Land Use Study Group, *Report on the University of Stirling* (1966), Stirling and Clackmannan County Councils.

Matthew, R., Johnson-Marshall & Partners, *University of Stirling: Interim Development Plan*, 1966.

Matthew, R., Johnson-Marshall & Partners, Population Projections, *Land Use Study Group Report*, 1966.

Matthew, R., Johnson-Marshall & Partners, University of Stirling, Development Plan, Report, 1968.

Meyer, J. R., 'Regional Economics', *Surveys of Economic Theory*, Vol. II, 1969.

Mishan, E. J. & Needleman, L., 'Immigration, Some Economic Effects', *Lloyds Bank Review*, July 1966.

The National Plan, 1965, Cmnd 2764.

Rennie, R. G. & Crowther-Gordon, T., 'The Counties of Stirling and Clackmannan', *Third Statistical Account of Scotland*, Vol. XVIII, 1966.

Report of a Committee on *Higher Education* under the Chairmanship of Lord Robbins, 1963, Cmnd 2154.

Report of a Committee on *The Intermediate Areas* under the Chairmanship of Sir John Hunt, 1969, Cmnd 3998.

Steele, D. B., 'Regional Multipliers in Great Britain', *Oxford Economic Papers*, July 1969.

Swift, B. M., 'Population', chapter 4, *The Lothians Regional Survey and Plan* Vol. 1, Glasgow University, 1966.

Weiss, S. J., and Gooding, E. C., 'Estimation of Differential Employment Multipliers', *Land Economics*, No. 44, 1968.

Wilson, T., 'The Regional Multiplier: A Critique', *Oxford Economic Papers*, November 1968.